Coping with Workplace Grief

Dealing with Loss, Trauma, and Change

Revised Edition

J. Shep Jeffreys, Ed.D., C.T.

A Crisp Fifty-Minute™ Series Book

This Fifty-Minute™ Book is designed to be "read with a pencil." It is an excellent workbook for self-study as well as classroom learning. All material is copyright-protected and cannot be duplicated without permission from the publisher. *Therefore, be sure to order a copy for every training participant by contacting:*

THOMSON

COURSE TECHNOLOGY

1-800-442-7477 ◆ 25 Thomson Place, Boston, MA ◆ www.courseilt.com

Coping with Workplace Grief

Dealing with Loss, Trauma, and Change

Revised Edition

J. Shep Jeffreys, Ed.D., C.T.

CREDITS:

Product Manager:	**Debbie Woodbury**
Editor:	**Ann Gosch**
Production Editor:	**Genevieve McDermott**
Production Artists:	**Nicole Phillips, Rich Lehl, and Betty Hopkins**
Manufacturing:	**Denise Powers and Melissa Hulse**

For more information contact:

Course Technology
25 Thomson Place
Boston, MA 02210

Or find us on the Web at **www.courseilt.com**

For permission to use material from this text or product, submit a request online at: www.thomsonrights.com

Any additional questions about permissions can be submitted by e-mail to: thomsonrights@thomson.com

Trademarks

Crisp Fifty-Minute Series is a trademark of Course Technology.

Some of the product names and company names used in this book have been used for identification purposes only and may be trademarks or registered trademarks of their respective manufacturers and sellers.

Disclaimer

Course Technology reserves the right to revise this publication and make changes from time to time in its content without notice.

ISBN 1-56052-676-9
Library of Congress Catalog Card Number 2005926707
Printed in Canada by Webcom Limited
1 2 3 4 5 PM 08 07 06 05

Learning Objectives for

COPING WITH
WORKPLACE GRIEF

The learning objectives for *Coping with Workplace Grief* are listed below. They have been developed to guide the user to the core issues covered in this book.

The objectives of this book are to help the user:

1) Identify sources of change in the workplace that may trigger feelings of loss or grief

2) Discover the impact of threatened or lost workplace attachments

3) Understand various reactions to workplace change caused by reorganization, downsizing, trauma, death, illness, impairment, and other actions outside their control

4) Learn how unacknowledged reactions to loss and grief can affect productivity

5) Acquire techniques for supporting people in grief, including recognizing when someone needs professional counseling

6) Recognize when they are experiencing reactions to change and explore techniques for dealing with their own sense of loss or grief

Assessing Progress

Course Technology has developed a Crisp Series **assessment** that covers the fundamental information presented in this book. A 25-item, multiple-choice and true/false questionnaire allows the reader to evaluate his or her comprehension of the subject matter.

To buy the assessment and answer key, go to www.courseilt.com and search on the book title or via the assessment format, or call 1-800-442-7477.

Assessments should not be used in any employee-selection process.

About the Author

John Shep Jeffreys, Ed.D., C.T., is a psychologist with a specialty in the treatment of grief-related problems, author, speaker and organizational consultant. He is an assistant professor of psychiatry at The Johns Hopkins University School of Medicine and affiliate assistant professor of pastoral counseling at Loyola College in Maryland. He is certified in Thanatology by the Association for Death Education and Counseling and has worked as a trainer and workshop leader with Elisabeth Kübler-Ross, M.D.

His consultation service, J. S. Jeffreys and Associates, offers organizational executives on-site support for managing workplace change and transition grief, and consultation for employee death and grief in the workplace.

In addition to this book, now in its second edition, Dr. Jeffreys is the author of *Helping People Grieve—When Tears Are Not Enough: A Handbook for Care Providers* (Brunner-Routledge, 2005). He can be reached at his Web site: www.GriefCareProvider.com or at jeffreys3@comcast.net.

Acknowledgments

No undertaking such as this book happens without very special help from others.

First, I acknowledge my teacher, the late Elisabeth Kübler-Ross, M.D., who enabled me to travel my own path of grief to healing and service to others.

Special thanks to management coach Richard Yocum for a detailed review of the manuscript and invaluable suggestions. To Laraine Pincus, Ph.D., for her excellent clinical review. To Helane Jeffreys, president of Voice for Success, for listening skills material, and to communications consultant Deborah Jeffreys Hurley for her pre-editing suggestions. To Ronald Jeffreys, D.O., for his guidance from a medical perspective.

Deepest appreciation to Roberta Israeloff, who provided her wonderful editorial insights into content style, form, and flow.

Dedication

This book is dedicated to my wife, Helane, whose vision initiated this project and who continues to be a loving guide and inspiration for this work.

Preface

Reading *Coping with Workplace Grief* may be your first step in taking control of a painful time in your life or in advising others whom you are in a position to help.

This book is designed to help you and others understand grief and take action to begin healing. We seldom have control over the losses we suffer. What we *can* control, however, is how we respond to change, loss, and grief. This book will provide you with an understanding of what grief is and how to better manage change, loss, and grief in the workplace.

Once you understand grief and how normal it is, you will never again think of it as unnecessary. You will not think of grieving as a sign of weakness or bad attitude. Grief is not right or wrong—it is just a natural human reaction to loss. The loss can be a death, a traumatic event, or some other important change in a person's employment or other life circumstances. Everyone grieves differently, and the timetable for mourning varies by individual. Managers, human resources staff, supervisors, co-workers, and others can help this process along by attending to two basic requirements: *to learn to honor and let go of what was* and *to facilitate new beginnings*.

Employees who are grieving often feel isolated. It is not easy to be close to another's pain. Watching other people deal with loss, trauma, and grief can easily trigger our own unfinished grief, which makes it harder for us to be with them. At the same time, we often do not know what to say or do.

Reaching out to someone in need is easier if we are able to acknowledge and vent our own stored grief with a trusted family member or colleague. It also helps to know what to expect from the grief reaction and to learn specific helping skills. In these ways, you can make a difference to an employee who is grieving.

I hope and trust that you will find this book helpful.

My very best wishes,

J. Shep Jeffreys

J. Shep Jeffreys, Ed.D., C.T.

Introduction

Let's face it. No one wants to deal with grief and pain. Many of us run away from people who are dealing with a tragic loss. We want to push loss from our minds because it is just too terrible to hear and think about. It scares us to imagine that the misfortune of others could also happen to us.

Grief is part of the human experience. It is our reaction to loss or the threat of loss, and it has its origin in a part of the brain whose job it is to keep us alive in times of danger. Grief shows up in many forms, and it can last for weeks, months, or years.

We usually associate grief with death and the loss of loved ones. But grief arises from many sources besides death and dying. For years, employees and their families have experienced as a death-like loss the traumatic changes and subsequent losses that have been taking place in the workplace. Many report ongoing stress symptoms from terrorism, military actions, national alerts, and other threats that raise our state of vigilance. The more you can anticipate feelings, attitudes, and behaviors caused by grief, the more comfortable you will be talking to a grieving employee or colleague.

Our grief is real. It is normal, and there are things we can do to help each other. That's what this book is about.

There are several basic myths that influence the way many people react to change, loss, and grief. You are probably already familiar with several of them.

Common Myths About Grief

> ➤ Bad things happen to *other* people

> ➤ I can handle this on my own

> ➤ I don't need to talk about it

> ➤ No one can tell how upset I really am

> ➤ My pain, anger, and fear will just go away on their own

> ➤ If I don't think about it or talk about it, then nothing happened or will happen

> ➤ Only positive feelings are okay to express during workplace change

The beliefs contained in these myths can get in the way of people's seeking and receiving the help and support they need to heal, adjust, and grow.

Seven Basic Principles of Grief

The seven principles of grief that follow are statements about how people grieve. An appreciation of these principles paves the way for support and understanding of grieving people.

1. **You cannot *fix* or cure grief.**

   Grief is not an illness. It is a combination of thoughts, physical and emotional feelings, and behaviors that are designed—believe it or not—to enable us to *survive*. Grief is therefore a normal way of reacting whenever we have already lost or are afraid we will lose someone or something important to us.

   Failure to acknowledge and prepare for employee-transition grief can result in major morale and productivity problems.

2. **Everyone grieves differently.**

   Some people put up a no-tears front but cry on the inside. Others are comfortable with crying in very visible ways. There is no *right* or *best* way to grieve.

3. **There is no set timetable for grief.**

   Many people ask, "How long will it take for me to move beyond my grief?" The answer is: "As long as it takes." Too often we do not give ourselves permission to do the grieving that will eventually result in healing and reclaiming of a life. Additionally, grievers are often pressured by others to "move on!" In some work settings, grieving is seen as a "bad attitude" by those who likewise want the person in grief to "move on."

4. **Every loss is a multiple loss.**

   We lose more than a person, more than a job, more than a building, or even a sense of well-being. We lose the part of ourselves that had interacted with that which is no more—the deceased; the workplace environment; the routines; the safe, joyful, or carefree fun times; and the hope and dreams for the future.

5. **Grief comes as a result of loss due to change: Change = Loss = Grief**

   Life is full of changes and necessary transitions that require us to let go of someone or something. We move from home to school and school to workplace, from being single to being a couple, to creating a family, to retirement—through each stage of adulthood. We are faced throughout our life with the potential for a grief reaction. Even the *threat* of a loss can activate a grief reaction.

6. **Grieving the loss of *what was* and reinvesting in *what will be* can eventually bring about growth and renewal.**

   When grieving people are acknowledged and supported, their healing is enhanced and they are then more likely to adjust to a new environment and grow.

7. **We grieve our old losses whenever we experience a new loss.**

   When a new loss occurs, the old grief mingles with the new and increases the intensity of the grief reaction.

Having previewed some basic features of grief, let's turn to sources of loss and grief in the workplace.

Table of Contents

Appendix 87

Sources of Loss and Grief in the Workplace

> *To exist is to change, to change is to mature, to mature is to go on creating oneself endlessly."*
>
> —Henri Bergson

Ongoing Workplace Change

"Change is good!" "I need a change!" "Things have to change!"

Everyone is talking about change. But *how much* change is good? And how often should it occur?

The work environment nowadays is described as "permanent white water." In other words, today's workplace is characterized by a series of swift and drastic changes in organizational structure, employment status, job descriptions, sources of labor, corporate names, supporting technology, markets, and physical locations. We can no longer assume that salaries, benefits, people, and a sense of safety and job security will stay as they have been.

Many business organizations have moved toward work teams and cut back on middle managers. And many no longer automatically guarantee their employees job security solely on the basis of loyalty and work well done. Workers are more and more often considered resources to be moved throughout or out of the organization as necessary. Increasingly, job continuation is determined by performance outcomes and short-term needs, rather than by more emotional factors such as company loyalty and seniority.

Many employees experience the profound changes in the workplace such as job loss, reassignment, or new management as if they have slipped through a crack in the universe and no longer recognize where or who they are. Changes in our lives create grief because we have lost what used to be. What was once a secure "home away from home" becomes a frightening, unfriendly, and even hostile workplace.

This book will help you cope with the specific changes you and your co-workers are experiencing. First, we will examine the major factors causing transformations in the business world. We will also review the ongoing grief reactions in the workplace due to disasters, co-worker death and serious illness, and the personal loss of colleagues. Then we will consider how these distressing changes affect employees and their families, managers, and the workplace family. This will be approached by providing an understanding of what to expect from people who are grieving and how managers and co-workers can help them.

Mergers, Layoffs, and Reorganization

In the wake of a changing work world, employees experience mergers and buyouts of companies, and these often result in layoffs for some and higher workloads for those surviving the layoffs. Lost in this process is a sense of predictability and control over our work lives.

Social and business networks may be disrupted. People in charge may lose their status. People who have worked in close proximity, who have bonded and served as emotional support for one another, may be separated. When people leave without an opportunity to say good-bye, those remaining report a sense of dread and end up distrusting management.

People who have lived through earthquakes and other natural disasters have their expectations about life shaken to the core. In a similar way, the foundation has been knocked out from under millions of employees who have experienced the ongoing "earthquakes" of organizational change.

When new leaders take over a company, many people lose their role in their work-life decision-making process. They may feel confused, bereft, angry, apathetic, and anxious and may suffer from such bodily symptoms as aches and pains, physical and mental slowdown, fatigue, and illness. The connection between these complaints and lowered productivity is well known.

Transition Grief for Layoff Survivors

After a change, new management often reduces the number of departments and staff and reorganizes and relocates those who are left. As a result, those surviving the layoffs have to cope with multiple changes: new reporting relationships, new work groups, new job descriptions, changes in the physical surroundings, new company, and a new corporate identity.

The net effect is a new culture with new expectations, routines, procedures, and people. Employees must accomplish two difficult tasks at once: adjust to a new work environment and let go of the way things used to be. Leaving the old workplace culture behind brings on transition grief.

Ironically, those who survive job layoffs often have a harder time adjusting than those who are let go. A survey of layoff "survivors," conducted by Anderson and Knowledge Systems & Research (CNN.com, August 24, 2000), reported that survivors were less satisfied with their companies' handling of the transition than were employees who were laid off. Fifty-three percent of survivors reported that their work responsibilities had increased in the six months following the downsizing.

Another nationwide survey of corporate representatives concluded that the same level of support and counseling that departing employees get must be made available to those remaining on the job (GHR Training Solutions, October, 2001).

Reorganizing a company, merging two or more corporate cultures, or scaling down existing operations represents a difficult transition and provides a challenge for those involved. "The way we were" is no longer part of the way we are now.

To fully understand the experience of grief in the workplace, take a moment to reflect on your own experiences or those of someone you know. Then complete the following two "discovery" exercises. They are designed to help you recall information that you already have stored in your mind.

WORKPLACE CHANGE-LOSS CHECKLIST

In this exercise you will look at your recollections of various changes in the workplace. Check (✓) the workplace changes experienced by you or someone you know well. Check the *M* column if it was your experience or the *O* column if it was another person's.

M = My experience   O = Other person

	M	O
Hostile takeover	❏	❏
Chapter 11/bankruptcy	❏	❏
Layoffs	❏	❏
Reorganization	❏	❏
Going out of business	❏	❏
Merger/acquisition	❏	❏
Downsizing/scaling	❏	❏
Redeployment/transfers	❏	❏
Change in technology system	❏	❏
Company relocation	❏	❏
Restructuring/flattening	❏	❏
Serious drop in business	❏	❏
Loss of CEO/other leaders	❏	❏
Outsourcing/competitive sourcing	❏	❏
Serious budget cuts	❏	❏

CONTINUED

CONTINUED

M = My experience   O = Other person

	M	O
Co-worker death	☐	☐
Co-worker serious illness	☐	☐
Fire, earthquake, or other destruction	☐	☐
Other: _____	☐	☐
Other: _____	☐	☐
Other: _____	☐	☐

Each workplace change event carries with it a multitude of possible reactions. As you recall each of the above experiences, try to remember any of the resulting reactions you or others had.

By linking workplace changes to employee reaction, you will begin to understand the following equation:

Change = Loss = Grief

Whenever we experience a change, we lose what we changed from. Routines, rhythms of our interaction with colleagues, identification with a unit or company name, new job descriptions, new location, and acute changes due to health or illness alter our activities drastically. The change or loss creates grief reaction, and this is normal, expected, and must be supported in the workplace in order for healing to take place.

WORKPLACE GRIEF REACTION CHECKLIST

What grief reactions to workplace change-loss have you observed? How does change affect you and your co-workers? For any of the items below that you have experienced or observed in others as a result of workplace change, check (✔) the number that best indicates the level of reaction that occurred.

1 = Very little   2 = Moderate amount   3 = Significant amount

1	2	3	
❑	❑	❑	Physical aches and pains
❑	❑	❑	Shouting
❑	❑	❑	Absenteeism
❑	❑	❑	Fear for personal safety
❑	❑	❑	Sleep or eating disturbance
❑	❑	❑	Alcohol/drug abuse
❑	❑	❑	Forgetfulness
❑	❑	❑	Work errors
❑	❑	❑	Apathy
❑	❑	❑	Filing of grievances
❑	❑	❑	Hoarding of supplies and resources
❑	❑	❑	Slow motion
❑	❑	❑	Panic attacks
❑	❑	❑	Fatigue
❑	❑	❑	Hostile conflicts, fighting
❑	❑	❑	Anxiety, worry
❑	❑	❑	Theft
❑	❑	❑	Tardiness

CONTINUED

| 1 = Very little | 2 = Moderate amount | 3 = Significant amount |

1	2	3	
❑	❑	❑	Self-blame
❑	❑	❑	Violent behavior
❑	❑	❑	Pessimism
❑	❑	❑	Anger, irritability
❑	❑	❑	Sabotage
❑	❑	❑	Hurt, crying
❑	❑	❑	Hyperactivity
❑	❑	❑	Isolation
❑	❑	❑	Distrust, suspicion
❑	❑	❑	Feelings of victimization
❑	❑	❑	Numbness
❑	❑	❑	Combat mentality
❑	❑	❑	Denial, avoidance
❑	❑	❑	Self-doubt

During periods of workplace change, what were the effects on productivity? (Check one.)

Productivity =   ❑ Much lower?   ❑ Same?   ❑ Higher?

How does this make you feel now? _____

_____

_____

The Effects of Workplace Change

Now that you have taken a look at your and others' grief reactions to change-loss, let's look at some cases that illustrate the effects of workplace change.

Case: "I'm the only one left!"

A worker who survived massive layoffs says: "They're all gone! And I never had a chance to say good-bye. They were told to talk to no one, to clean out their desks, and to leave immediately. That was a week ago. Today, I look around the large, open office, and all I see are empty workstations. My heart sinks all over again. At first I tried to ignore this feeling, but I can't. The place looks so different. And I feel so guilty and afraid. Why?

This person, a survivor, cannot get past the feelings of loss. The workplace has been irrevocably changed and the mourning process has begun.

Case: "Where do I belong?"

A woman who has worked in her company for 12 years says: "I don't know who I am when I come to work these days. Things are so different since the reorganization. I have a new office, a new supervisor. Even the company itself has a new name. I didn't think it would be so bad, but I find myself crying a few minutes after I get here."

This woman is experiencing a conflict between her picture of herself and the job requirements of her new work environment. She does not envision herself fitting into the new organizational arrangement.

> **Case: "I'm relieved but also afraid."**
>
> A recently unemployed man says: "Now that I've been laid off, it's not as bad as I thought it would be. For 18 months, I've been waiting for the other shoe to drop. Not knowing if I would be out of a job, and fearing that I would be, kept my emotions on edge. I can't describe how tense I constantly felt. I had many physical symptoms as well. When it finally happened, I was almost relieved. Even after six months of not working, I'm still not as anxious as I was while I was waiting to be laid off. But now I'm battling depression. I just don't know what will happen next."

The grieving process begins with the threat of loss. For many people, like this man, anxiety sets in the moment they hear the first rumors whispering of merger, downsizing, and reorganization. Many employees live with constant anxiety. Their experience is similar to those of people who are waiting for the results of a biopsy or blood test. Both situations could mean a death or a death-like loss.

Look back at these three cases. You could probably add several of your own from workplace experiences you or others have had. List them below. Circle those that you yourself experienced.

1. _____

_____

_____

2. _____

_____

_____

3. _____

_____

_____

Co-Worker Deaths, Accidents, and Disasters

In addition to the loss and grief attributed to organizational change, grieving also comes from co-worker deaths, accidents, and workplace disasters. The effect of a co-worker's serious illness or death can be similar to the loss or threatened loss of a person's own family member or friend.

Almost 6,000 people died on the job from fatal accidents in 2000 (Bureau of Labor Statistics). Many more deaths each year are due to illness, homicide, and suicide, while still other co-workers are diagnosed with life-threatening medical conditions.

Nowadays we also must add employee reactions to the losses of lives, businesses, buildings, customers, and suppliers that come from acts of terrorism and workplace violence, such as the 9/11 attacks, the Oklahoma City bombing, or mass shootings. The overwhelming impact of such assaults re-triggers grief among those already grieving loss in the workplace. Anxiety is also heightened as stories, facts, and new threats emerge.

For those directly and indirectly affected, grief and fear may be long-term realities of returning to the workplace. Employee surveys verify the stated and unstated fears about being safe in high-profile buildings, traveling to work over bridges or through tunnels, and simply spending the workday in a densely populated area.

When co-workers die or become seriously ill, our own fears of death may be forced into our minds and add to the level of grief and anxiety. Still, our reactions to a co-worker's death from an illness or other causes unrelated to the workplace are less likely to be as stressful as they are for unexpected, traumatic death.

A bombing, workplace violence, or a devastating non-work illness or death ends a familiar world and thrusts us into a new one. As previously noted, death and destruction violate the world we have always known and had expected to continue, jolting us out of our old ways of coping. Such massive and rapid change makes us realize that we cannot reasonably predict what will happen next. It fills many people with alarm and grief. Others learn to cope with an underlying level of stress, anxiety, and grief as a backdrop in their lives. All of these normal feelings, concerns, and disturbances are brought into the workplace.

No matter what the nature and number of the deaths, the organization must have a plan to deal with employees' needs, provide rituals of acknowledgment, and grant appropriate time off for mourning the death of colleagues.

Case Study: The Aftereffects of Disaster

"I am afraid to come to work." "Things are so uncertain." "Our company is planning to move to a safer location." "I find myself being startled easily." "I have no desire to get into the workload." "Everyone is on edge about what might happen next." "Nothing will ever be the same."

The horror of memories of a fire, flood, or human-made disaster and the continuing possibility of additional loss leave people with ongoing anxiety symptoms—sleeplessness, bad dreams, appetite disturbances, nervousness and jumpiness, heart palpitations, and various aches and pains. These have a direct effect on morale, motivation, attendance, and productivity.

Please list the changes you noted earlier on the Workplace Change-Loss Checklist that you yourself have experienced.

1. _____
2. _____
3. _____
4. _____
5. _____

As you complete the readings and exercises in this book, you can refer to these workplace changes as the source of your own grief reactions.

The Stages of Workplace Transformation

We have looked at the causes of multiple changes in the workplace. These are listed in columns 1, 2, and 3 in the following table. The other three columns outline the evolution individuals go through from the impact itself to the ultimate positive outcome—healing and growth.

1	2	3	4	5	6
Massive Impacts	Workplace Upheaval	Employee Changes/Loss	Grief Reaction	Transition/ Adjustment	Healing & Growth
Markets Technology Globalization Disasters	Layoffs Mergers Bankruptcies Outsourcing Deaths and Illness	Colleagues Location Security Trust	Feelings Attitudes Behaviors	Four Tasks of Healing Grief	Employee & Organizational Adaptation

Let's take a look at each of these six stages in more detail.

1. Massive Impacts

Transformations in organizational goals and operations have in the past been largely due to:

> ➤ Technological advances

> ➤ Globalization of corporate operations

> ➤ Changes in global and national market competition

Throughout the final decade of the past century and into the beginning of the present one, business failures, a plunging stock market, and threats of terrorism have all sent shock waves throughout our many and varied workplaces. The actions taken by corporations to survive have created constant and far-reaching waves of change that move through the organizational chart to all personnel.

2. Workplace Upheaval

The results of these waves of change—downsizing, mergers, restructuring and reorganization, redeployment, relocation, outsourcing, and bankruptcy—are now an ongoing part of the business picture. In other words, we are experiencing *traumatic transitions*—which is further accelerated by dramatic shifts from traditional hierarchical management structures to a "cluster" or work-team organization.

Managers become coaches and team leaders rather than bosses. Job descriptions are changed or expanded and require new skills. Staff and other resources are scarce, but the same output is still expected. Many employees are doing the work of laid-off colleagues in addition to their existing jobs. More decisions are made at the work-team level and fewer by general managers. Offices are relocated, co-workers are left behind, and familiar routines and cherished equipment and instruments are lost to the workplace change. Fear and uncertainty about the future is the name of the game.

Added to these changes is the nagging issue of safety and security both at work and at home. Additional and dramatic security and safety measures are visible in many work settings and serve as constant reminders that there is a level of uncertainty we must live with.

3. Employee Changes/Loss

Loss and the resulting grief are products of change in the workplace, and this affects employees at all levels.

Perhaps the most overlooked consequences of the turbulent changes in the corporate world, beginning in the 1980s, are the human factors of loss and grief. How does workplace change become workplace loss and grief? Whatever we left behind after we went through the transition represents loss. Even if the new situation is a desired change—promotion, new office—we still *lose* the way it used to be, and the reaction to this loss is grief.

When a company alters its organization by reducing or redeploying its workforce, or makes other substantial changes in the way it meets its goals, employees experience the loss of what used to be:

- ➤ People with whom they have bonded
- ➤ Status in the organization
- ➤ Control over their work
- ➤ Familiar procedures and surroundings
- ➤ Trusted reporting relationships
- ➤ Certainty about their future
- ➤ Their own assumptions about what could be expected from the company

Survivors of layoffs and reorganizations react with feelings similar to those of people who are grieving a death or the diagnosis of life-threatening illness.

Similarly, the proliferation of metal detectors and beefed-up security forces and the searching of bags and briefcases when we come to work remind us that we have also lost our sense of well-being.

Whenever there is change, there is loss, and loss always brings about some degree of grief reaction. Our society in general, and the business world specifically, has typically not granted enough permission for people to grieve. As a result, many grieving employees are given little time to be off balance, sad, angry, scared, unmotivated, and unproductive. When there is a lack of time to mourn what was, employees are less free to bond to the new situation. Grieving people need to be acknowledged, and this can be done in the workplace by use of rituals, newsletters, e-letters, and providing opportunities for EAP or other grief counseling resources.

4. Grief Reaction

Death and serious illness as well as change and loss in the workplace result in grief in the workplace. This generates feelings, attitudes, and behaviors that are normal and expected responses to grief.

When companies change to "lean and mean," people become sad, angry, and frightened about the future. Their attitudes and behaviors reflect this. For example, work output usually suffers for some time. Managers and human resources staff report that employees seek increased time off, have more medical complaints, and adopt a generally apathetic or "what's the use" mood. Increased errors and accidents, decreased efficiency and creative problem-solving, sabotage, and violence have also been reported.

The above reactions are also true where employee death, serious illness, or physical impairment have occurred. It is very important that managers and employees be sensitive to deaths and serious illness that take place in the personal lives of co-workers. The workplace group frequently takes on the role of a family system and the reactions and support of work friends and management play an important role in helping grieving colleagues and facilitating the healing needed to return to a productive life. Be aware also that many employees become family caregivers for a loved one in the aftermath of a serious accident or due to illness, physical damage, and/or mental impairment. Managers should be sensitive to the effects on mood, energy level, and occasional time required to be away from the workplace for caregiving requirements.

News of death, accident, or the diagnosis of a serious illness should be communicated to the staff as soon as possible. Employees should be given time off to attend funerals, make hospital visits, and communicate with the family. It is sometimes necessary to have an Employee Assistance Counselor or an outside mental health specialist provide group and/or individual assistance. Grief is a normal reaction and is always stressful.

A *Wall Street Journal* article (August 10, 1994) stated that companies ignoring employees' stress "pay in absenteeism, efficiency, and morale problems." This remains true today.

5. Transition and Adjustment to Change

Workplace grief is no different from any other grief. To reduce human suffering and the negative effects of grief on work, organizations must:

> ➤ Know what to anticipate in grief reactions

> ➤ Allow sufficient time for grieving, including adequate leave for mourning

> ➤ Actively support employees through the *Four Tasks of Healing*

Grief reactions do not go away; they go underground and decrease morale and productivity.

6. Healing and Growth

Healing through grief in the workplace benefits individual employees and the organization. When companies acknowledge employees' grief reactions and support people through the transition, grief is less intense, and the negative effects on their ability to work are diminished. The goal of all organizations should be to provide for healing and transformation to the new work setting and its requirements.

Even employees who are not directly involved in events leading to changes and loss in an organization may have continuing stress and grief reactions. They will require understanding and support from their managers for what may be an uncertain period. When employees are supported through the grief process, they can begin to regain their balance and return to a productive work life.

Employees will take notice of how a grieving co-worker is treated by management, and how the work requirements are balanced with the needs of a mourning colleague. The usual policy of three-day bereavement leave can be augmented by pooled and donated leave time or special arrangements for initial reduced workload. Providing private space for grieving as needed and access to EAP counselors also demonstrate a supportive, caring workplace environment and produce a typically positive staff reaction to management.

In the *Workplace Change-Loss History* on the next page, you will have an opportunity to inventory some important workplace loss or change events that have affected you.

YOUR WORKPLACE CHANGE-LOSS HISTORY

To review your own firsthand experience with workplace change, complete the following exercise.

Choose the three most important workplace changes that you have experienced. Write down what was upsetting about each event and also what was eventually positive about the change cited.

Change 1: _____

_____

What was upsetting? _____

_____

What was positive? _____

_____

Change 2: _____

_____

What was upsetting? _____

_____

What was positive? _____

_____

Change 3: _____

_____

What was upsetting? _____

_____

What was positive? _____

_____

Take a moment to jot down what may still be left over for you about any of the items above. It can be very helpful to discuss this with a trusted friend or a family member. If you find that you have been thinking about these items a lot, you may wish to consult an EAP counselor.

PART 2

The Complexities

of Grief

Attachment, Bonding, and Loss

"I struggled against the ocean current, which was pulling me into the jutting rocks of the breaker. I worked hard to resist the urge to just give in and not try anymore. My son tried a rescue from a rubber raft, but I waved him away, fearing he would be crushed against the rocks. My heart was pounding! I felt utterly exhausted and my resolve to survive was fading. I heard myself saying, 'Is this it? The end?' Somehow I managed to reach through the exhaustion and grasp the edge of a rock and hold on for dear life—long enough to gain the strength to pull myself up onto the top of the breaker ledge and to safety."

The instinct for survival—to hang on for dear life—is a basic human drive. Baby animals literally cling to their mother's fur. People hang on to their self-image, each other, routines, dreams, favorite things, and job titles. These are examples of the attachment theory developed by John Bowlby, M.D., who studied the way babies and small children acted when they were separated from their mothers (Bowlby, 1980).

We attach early to a mother or mother substitute to survive. And the attachment behaviors—staying close, hanging on, reaching for the person or other object of attachment—continue throughout life. Attachment behavior leads to the creation of attachment bonds. The way we make and break bonds in the early part of our lives determines how we will deal with connecting and letting go later in life.

Psychologists have studied the way adults bond to each other and found that the same drive for survival plays an important role in connecting with each other as life partners, family members, colleagues, and friends. This basic, primitive attachment-for-survival is the energy source that underlies every bond that is formed. That is why we may panic when we feel on the brink of losing someone or something that we care very much about. It can feel as threatening to our survival as an infant's separation from its mother.

Sigmund Freud wrote that we not only mourn for the loss of tangible bonds, such as the loss of people, but we also grieve for the loss of such intangibles as self-image, dreams, and health (Freud, 1917). We begin to grieve as soon as there is a hint that a bond is threatened.

To help you explore your own attachments in the workplace, complete the *Workplace Attachment Survey* on the following page.

WORKPLACE ATTACHMENT SURVEY

To help you understand the needs that your job is meeting for you, list the five most important aspects of your current work role. What would you miss the most if you were transferred or if the job were significantly changed?

Current job title: _____

What features of my job would I hate to lose most? List these in the numbered spaces below. You may be surprised to realize that there are aspects of your job you would not want to lose. Ask yourself what it is about each feature that makes you want to hold on to it. Write your answers on the line that follows each aspect you listed.

1. _____

   _____

2. _____

   _____

3. _____

   _____

4. _____

   _____

5. _____

   _____

Defining Grief and Its Causes

As you have learned, feelings of loss are rooted in primitive attachment-for-survival instincts. Intellectually, we know that suffering most losses will not actually threaten our very survival, but loss can *feel* that way, leading to a grief reaction. But just what is grief?

Grief is defined as *a set of reactions to loss or the threat of loss of a bond or connection* to someone or something. Grief includes feelings, attitudes, and behaviors that exist over a period of time. Grief may also include physical symptoms, confusion, memory difficulties, and problems with concentration. The nature and duration of the grief reactions vary greatly.

Three Causes of Grief

An actual loss is not the only condition that leads to feelings of grief. People also grieve during the *threat* of a loss and for *something they never had and never will have*. Let's examine these three causes of grief more closely.

Loss

We grieve when we *lose* something: a loved one, a pet, a job, our wallet, workplace friends, a familiar role in the organization, the old "family" atmosphere at work, our identity in the workplace, peace of mind. Whenever a bond is broken or significantly altered, the grief reaction begins.

The Threat of a Loss

We grieve when we are *threatened with the loss* of something or the possibility of significantly altering a bond: having a biopsy or other medical tests, waiting for a child who is late coming home from school, hearing rumors of layoffs, or learning that top-level management is meeting with known competitors.

> **Case: A Perceived Loss**
>
> In a company whose financial situation was known to be shaky because several large contracts went to competitors, a mid-level manager experienced severe stress-related symptoms—insomnia, loss of appetite, inability to concentrate, and a sense of dread each morning. He was able to pinpoint the onset of these symptoms to the first time he became aware that his boss was not his usual friendly self. Instead of warm, familiar conversation, there was now formal, abrupt communication. This alteration in their relationship bred a slow panic for the middle manager. In his mind he began to create "what if" and "suppose that" scenarios. Then came the sick feeling in his stomach that indicated the beginning of the grief reaction.

Something We Never Had and Never Will Have

Can you experience the "loss" of something you *never had and never will have*? Yes. What this condition represents is a perceived failure to bond or the loss of an opportunity to connect with a person or desired situation.

Some people, for example, grieve for the relationship they never had with their alcoholic mother or a brother who died in a war, an education never acquired, the career never attained, a dream lifestyle never achieved. A company's financial reverses and the resultant changes often contribute directly to the loss of dreams for not only the employees themselves but also for their families. What we do not get to have because of workplace trauma, change, and uncertainty creates multiple grief reactions.

> **Case: Facing Many Losses**
>
> Tom and Sue were planning a second child and were house-hunting for a bigger home. Tom had been a foreman at his plant for seven years and was known as a hard worker and loyal team player. He had taken courses in business and management at the local community college and knew that he was being considered for promotion to assistant manager. When his company was bought out by an aggressive competitor, Tom was notified by his manager that his division was to be reorganized and that new work teams would replace the current subgroups. Team leaders were being sent in from the new company's headquarters, and Tom would have to take a team member role or there would be no place for him in the new organization. He would no longer be reporting to his old boss and would share a desk out in the production area. There would be no change in benefits, and his salary would be slightly reduced.
>
> Tom is now faced with multiple real and threatened losses: of his immediate career development plans, his desired new home, his role and title of foreman, his reporting relationship with a friendly and supportive boss, and his own little office.

There are many people like Tom who, because of family needs, a poor job market, or fear of making a change, never get the education, the promotion, or the lifestyle they had hoped for. These missing pieces provide a continuous source of grief for employees and their families. Keep in mind that employees' families grieve along with them. Grief reaction affects the family and the workplace and can intensify until some help is given or something breaks down. Lack of professional help can result in communication and relationship breakdown.

TEST YOUR RECALL ON THE NATURE OF GRIEF

By completing this exercise, you can test yourself on how well you understand attachment, bonding, and grief.

1. What is the fundamental purpose of attachment and bonding? _____

_____

_____

_____

_____

2. In addition to people, what else do we bond to? _____

_____

_____

_____

_____

3. List the three conditions under which a person will grieve.

a. _____

b. _____

c. _____

Compare your answers to the author's suggestions in the Appendix.

Why All Loss Is Like a Death

We expect people to behave in a certain way when a loved one dies or is given six months to live. We also expect grief when a pet dies. People have reported that they "cried and cried" when they found out their father was diagnosed with Alzheimer's and was "no longer the dad I've always known." We understand grieving for these losses.

But "death" comes in many forms. We experience a death whenever something "we have always known to be" comes to an end. This is the loss that comes from change—planned or unexpected.

When a person we care about dies, a painful change takes place. When we move away from a home and neighborhood in which we have lived for several years, we may feel a similar pain for this death-like loss of friends and familiar surroundings, such as favorite shopping centers and parks.

A sense of loss also is created by traumatic events such as natural or manmade disasters or threats. These experiences leave us with prolonged anxiety, irritability, hyperactivity or numbness, withdrawal from others, upsetting dreams, aches and pains, and flashbacks during which the trauma is experienced again.

In the wake of the terrorist attacks at home and overseas, we may grieve the death of a seemingly safer world in which we once lived and for which we now yearn. Though our reactions may seem abnormal, they are, in fact, natural and normal survival behaviors. Many people react this way whenever our nation or community is threatened with danger from some outside force.

Losing the comfort of a safe and reliable work environment creates an ongoing sense of the loss of trust. Loss is the factor that determines our grief. Loss—whether from a death or a death-like change in our life circumstances—hurts.

To get a sense of the variety of loss affecting us, please complete the *Many Faces of Loss* on the next page. When you finish, take a moment to jot down the losses that bother you the most and write down why you think this is so.

THE MANY FACES OF LOSS

Loss has many faces: illness, aging, separation from people and places, unrealized dreams, dashed hopes for the future.

In the diagram below, write in the balloons any of the losses that you have experienced. Add any additional losses in the spaces provided below.

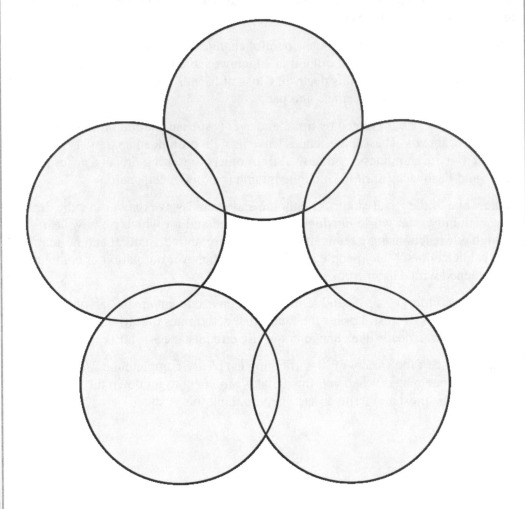

Add additional losses:

1. _____

2. _____

3. _____

Different Tears for Different Peers

Although all loss is like a death, the nature and duration of the grief reaction can vary greatly among people. Indeed, there is no one *right way* to grieve a loss. You have likely observed that some people cry openly at a time of sorrow, while others appear free of emotion. In the workplace, some employees will want to talk about their grief; others will keep their feelings to themselves. Some tears are on the outside, and some are on the inside.

A person may go in and out of grief reaction, experiencing periodic waves of sadness, anger, and fear. Some individuals will need many weeks or months to work through grief and reach a place of healing and resolution. Others seem to grieve forever. Still others who have experienced loss show no grief reactions at all and deny any internal grief feelings.

It is okay to grieve when you have experienced a loss. How much and how long is influenced by three factors:

➤ Your personality and your loss history

➤ The nature of the current loss

➤ The support you receive during the grieving process

These factors cannot necessarily help you predict your own or anyone's grief reaction. However, they can help you understand the differences in grieving among people. Let's look at each factor in more detail.

Personality and Loss History

The way people have made and broken bonds in the past will influence how they respond to a current loss. Those who have a history of successfully letting go of attachments will have the skills needed to get through the grief process and redirect their lives. Old, unresolved loss will complicate the grieving process. An employee may be overwhelmed with feelings from an old loss when a new loss has occurred.

Current physical or psychological distress will affect an employee's ability to grieve and heal. For example, employees with existing depression and physical ailments may find their grief aggravated.

Nature of the Current Loss

To support another's grieving, it is helpful to understand the nature of the grief being experienced. The following questions will help to clarify the extent and significance of losses and the resulting feelings being expressed:

➢ **How many actual losses are involved?**

A job transfer may mean more than losing surroundings and people. Routines, status, resource networks, easy parking, and even the friendly cook in the cafeteria may be left behind. A death, serious illness, or tragic accident in the family will have a rippling effect on the employee as well as on co-workers creating *a multiple loss*.

➢ **What is at risk?**

Change in the workplace may place career advancement at risk. It can open up many questions such as "Who am I in this reorganized workplace?" and "Am I still a valuable employee?" Death of a trusted co-worker or of a loved one can alter how an employee views him or herself in the post-loss workplace.

➢ **Is there an end in sight?**

After workplace changes or trauma, many employees ask themselves, "Will I ever be safe and secure here again?" If there seems to be no end in sight, the grief process can be prolonged. But knowing there is a light at the end of the tunnel helps the grief process move along. There is no universal timetable for grief regardless of the loss involved. It takes as long as it takes but the grieving person can be helped to heal with good support from workplace friends and community.

Support During the Grief Process

In the case of organizational transition: The more information and support an employee receives before and during a planned change, the less intense the grief response will be. The same is true when specialized help is available after unexpected catastrophes occur. In general, without the provision of information and grief support programs, management may be perceived as unsympathetic and uncaring.

Organizations run the risk of prolonging grief, which results in low morale and diminished productivity, when they fail to provide the workforce with advance notice of upcoming change. For best results, the *information flow should be ongoing* throughout the transition process, and employees must be granted sufficient time to heal through the grief process. Too often the expectation is that within a very few days, people are expected to bounce back into a productive, motivated level of job performance. The expectation should be that there will be some lag in productivity as the workforce heals and creates new ways of seeing themselves in the post-change work environment.

Help from family, friends, clergy, or other resources, also provides the employee with strength and stability during the transition-grief process. If employees are not getting support from loved ones or experience conflict and a lack of understanding at home, they may feel an increase in isolation and vulnerability. This can also extend the grieving and delay healing. Employee assistance counselors can help with this.

In the case of employee personal loss: Support from managers for employees must include an opportunity for the grieving staff member to have time to talk and express how he or she is feeling. The manager can facilitate needed time off beyond the customary three-day bereavement leave policies and work out temporary reduced workloads. Expect fatigue, anger, tears, a need to talk, or a need to keep private. A drop in productivity may result, but communicate faith in return to productive levels of work. Where the employee is seriously ill or tragically or physically impaired, seek assistance from an EAP counselor to provide support for co-workers. Provide human resources help with leave time, disability, and other paperwork. Remember, *grief travels across the workplace doorstep.*

In the case of the death of an employee: Send a clear message of sympathy and support to the other employees. The workplace is often an extended family and as such there may be a full range of grief reactions. These reactions may include old unfinished loss and grief issues for staff members. Arrange for staff to attend death-associated rituals, funerals, and family visitation. Support remembrance activities and workplace rituals. Where death occurred at the workplace and was witnessed by co-workers, there may be a need for help from EAP staff or other mental health professionals. Where the death was violent, special provisions will need to be made for specialists in post-trauma reactions. Help employees cope with increases in workload and be prepared for pain, confusion, anger, anxiety, and apathy.

Some things grieving employees want most:

➤ A good listener who doesn't give advice

➤ Flexibility with leave time and workload

➤ Time and space to grieve

➤ Visits and calls from colleagues

➤ Specific offers of help

➤ Attendance at funerals

➤ Being invited to lunch and other social events

➤ Donation of leave time

➤ Opportunities to grieve together

➤ A hug

In the *Change-Loss* exercise on the next page, you will have an opportunity to review some personal loss experiences and rate the current effect these are having on you. When our own loss and grief material is very noticeable, we will be limited in how much we can help others who are grieving.

YOUR CHANGE-LOSS HISTORY

The more you are aware of your own loss experience, the better you will be able to cope with grief, whether it is your own or a co-worker's. This exercise will help you to identify your own past grief reactions and their current effects.

In the spaces provided, write down three losses you can remember from childhood to the present. These can be a death, loss of a pet, loss of a work or other role, or any loss due to an important change in your life. Then circle the number that best indicates how much each loss remains a part of your thoughts and feelings.

Not much current thought or feelings   **Constant current thought or feelings**

Loss 1: _____

| 0 | 1 | 2 | 3 | 4 | 5 | 6 | 7 | 8 | 9 | 10 |

Loss 2: _____

| 0 | 1 | 2 | 3 | 4 | 5 | 6 | 7 | 8 | 9 | 10 |

Loss 3: _____

| 0 | 1 | 2 | 3 | 4 | 5 | 6 | 7 | 8 | 9 | 10 |

After you have completed the above, take a moment to recall the circumstances surrounding the loss that you scored with the highest rating.

What was helpful for you at the time of loss?

_____

_____

_____

What was not helpful for you at this time?

_____

_____

_____

CONTINUED

If you were a child, what did you hear from adults about loss and the expression of grief?

_____

_____

_____

_____

Compare your reactions to more recent loss with the way you handled loss in the past. Make a note on any differences you have identified.

_____

_____

_____

_____

Now that you have inventoried some of your own past losses, you may see that the nature and duration of your grief reactions have been tempered by experience. Experience, however, may not substantially change the behaviors of mourning.

The next sections explore what most people typically go through on their way to "moving on."

Bowlby's Basic Phases of Loss and Mourning

Much has been written about the nature of human grief, and one of the most influential writers is John Bowlby, M.D. (1907-1990). His findings, along with those of Elisabeth Kübler-Ross, M.D. (which follow this section), will give you an understanding of what to expect when working with employees in grief.

Dr. Bowlby studied the reactions of very young children to separation from their mothers. He developed an outline of what was observed as a result of this separation (Bowlby, 1980). He found that these descriptions also applied to adults who suffered loss.

As you learned earlier, attachment and bonding are instinctive behaviors. That is, we are born with them, and they are critical for survival. This is directly applicable to the grief reactions of adults dealing with any significant loss. Thus, the survival instinct causes every loss or threat of loss to activate a primitive drive to reconnect with that which was lost. When there is no way to reattach or reestablish the bond, the human grief response is triggered.

Bowlby identified several phases of the grieving process. Keep in mind that people vary in their individual grief reactions and that you may not necessarily experience the phases of grief in the sequence Bowlby described. See if you can recognize your own grief patterns or those of others you know.

Phase I: Numbness and Shutdown

This may last from a few hours to several weeks and can be interrupted by intense distress and/or anger. The person feels little or no pain at first and this is followed by distress, agitation, and/or anxiety over the separation.

Phase II: Protest

This phase involves protesting the loss and attempting to recover what was lost. This is a time of yearning for the lost object or situation, despite a lack of hope for recovery of what was lost. It is a time of anxiety and wishful thinking about what was lost. The grieving person seeks ways to deny or avoid the painful reality of loss.

Phase III: Disorganization/Despair

Despair sets in as hope fades for recovery of what was lost. This is a period of longing, apathy, hostility, and sadness. It is a breaking down of the old bonds, disorganization, pulling away, and mourning. Phase III is critical to the growth and healing in the next phase.

Phase IV: Detachment/Reorganization

This occurs after letting go of the attachment bond as it used to be. Active grieving—acknowledging and expressing the feelings and mental disruption described above—has taken place. The individual's energy is now redirected to new beginnings that may include carrying the lost person or situation within the heart. The grieving behaviors expressed in Phase III must occur to help people reach this phase of reorganization. This is why grief support is so vital to healing and restoring productivity.

Implications for the Workforce

Bowlby's phases make it clear that a complex set of reactions occurs after a separation or loss. Employees may attempt to recover what was lost by holding on to old work equipment, resisting a move to a new office location, lunching only with former colleagues, filing grievances and other actions to stop change, and engaging in other forms of written and vocal protest.

When employees are actively feeling and expressing grief emotions—anger, hurt, fear, guilt, shame—they have entered Bowlby's disorganization/despair phase. This is a time of decreased work effort and increased emotional and physical complaints.

Employees who survive an organizational transition or experience a tragic personal loss must undergo a period of grief and despair. This is a necessary and valuable part of the grief journey. Their expression of grief emotions enables them to let go of how things used to be and begin to direct energy to new beginnings. This is the period in which organizational help—workplace support programs—is critical.

During the detachment/reorganization phase, employees begin to look ahead to a new picture. They envision the end of the transition and begin to wonder, "Who am I?" This is the next part of their *healing-through-grief* journey, and it requires a new identity. It is a time for an inventory of skills and the development of new skills. It may even be a time during which employees set new work and career objectives.

Where there has been a death or diagnosis of a serious illness, employees will have had an opportunity to grieve and have their grief acknowledged by co-workers and management. The permission to express the pain and other feelings of grief and the opportunity to gradually create new ideas about their world without the lost loved one or colleague makes it possible to heal and return to more productive levels of work performance.

To help expand your understanding of the process of how people grieve, complete the following exercise.

RECOGNIZING THE PHASES OF GRIEF

To help expand your understanding of how people grieve, complete the following exercise.

Think of someone *outside* of the workplace that you know well—a family member, friend, or acquaintance—who has had a loss to deal with. Describe what the person did or said in each of Bowlby's Phases of Grief.

Briefly describe the loss situation:

_____

_____

Numbness/Shutdown Phase:

_____

_____

_____

Protest Phase:

_____

_____

_____

Disorganization/Despair Phase:

_____

_____

_____

Detachment/Reorganization Phase:

_____

_____

_____

We are now ready to look at another set of observations of how grieving people think, feel, and behave.

Kübler-Ross Descriptions of Reactions to Loss

Elisabeth Kübler-Ross, M.D. (1926-2004), first introduced the concepts of death and dying as a normal part of life in her well-known book, *On Death and Dying* (1969). She originally observed five categories of reactions when she studied dying cancer patients. Subsequently, these have been applied to most loss situations, including loss in the workplace. The five categories Kübler-Ross observed closely parallel the behaviors reported by employees coping with impending change in their work lives. The five reactions are:

Denial	*"No! Not me!" "It can't be!"*
Anger	*"Why me?" "Not fair!"*
Bargaining	*"Not yet!" "What can I do?"*
Depression	*"Go away!" "I'm too tired."*
Acceptance	*"Okay." "If that's the only way."*

Although Bowlby described the grief process as a succession of separate phases, Kübler-Ross's five stages are clusters of behavioral descriptions that can occur in any sequence. Understanding these will help you to further understand the normal reactions of human beings to loss or the threat of loss. Remember that not all people experience all of these behaviors, nor do they necessarily occur in this sequence. Let's take a look at each of these categories more closely.

Denial

"Oh no!" "I don't want to hear it!" Employees engaged in denial typically change the subject when conversations about workplace change come up. They push away thoughts about the painful reality and continue to use old forms, procedures, and labels. They may also stick with the "old guard" at lunchtime and keep a distance from the "new people."

We act this way when we do not want to let go of what has been so much a part of who and how we have been—co-workers, a sense of safety and trust, routines, and surroundings. To let go is to allow a part of *ourselves* to die. This is painful and we want to delay it, push it away, and pretend it isn't happening. We hope for a last-minute rescue, a change of heart by the board of directors, or a miraculous new contract.

Denial is a powerful tool and serves an important function when a loss is about to happen or has already occurred. Loss or the threat of loss is painful to think about, and no one wants pain. For many, deflecting the reality of the loss makes it possible to gather needed inner adjustment skills.

News of a death or frightening medical diagnosis is usually met with some form of denial. People actually hold their hands up with palms outward and physically push the bad news away. Denial acts as a shock absorber that allows the upsetting news to seep in slowly.

Although people are often criticized for being "in denial," some period of denial is natural and expected during the early stages of grieving a loss. There is no exact timetable for when denial should end. It will vary for each type of change-loss and for each person. As discussed earlier, our own history of making and breaking bonds will shape the way we deal with loss in the present.

Anger

"Why me?" "It's not fair!" "Why now, after all these years?!" "How could they do this?" "I hate them for this!" Rage, resentment, bitterness, sabotage, and violence can represent the anger phase of loss and grief.

Anger due to loss or threat of loss can be displaced to someone or something other than the source of the anger. When a loved one dies or receives a life-threatening diagnosis, the anger may be directed toward a higher being, a doctor, or the government. Loss in the workplace can prompt employees to dump their anger on the old management, the new management, co-workers, their family, or even the family pet.

Anger may be expressed directly as a hostile attitude, through words or behavior. Employees may also express their anger through grumbling, excessive questioning, complaining, angry facial expressions, arguing, fighting, insubordination, destruction of property, theft, physical violence, and sometimes homicide. Anger can also be expressed in passive or indirect ways. Lateness, absenteeism, work slowdown, increased errors, decreased cooperation, lack of follow-through, and diminished self-direction are examples of passive aggression.

For many people, grief as anger can be triggered over and over again as new developments in the loss that caused the anger are reported. For example, an executive who was fired by his employer may have his anger stirred up again merely by reading a notice about his replacement in the newspaper. Those experiencing continuous signs of resentment, irritability, and conflicts may need longer or more intensive group and individual support.

Bargaining

"Maybe if I come in earlier and stay later I'll survive the next layoff." "Can we keep these procedures for a little while longer?" "Is there any way that I can keep my office? My desk? My parking space?" "I'll even work for less money if I can stay in my old division." "Can we still use the old software for the established accounts?"

When faced with loss, people usually try to keep their attachments to their former work environment as intact as they can. In the face of life-threatening illness, people may bargain with their Creator and promise to pray regularly, eat healthier, quit smoking or drinking, exercise, be nicer, and generally improve their lifestyle.

Depression

"I feel like someone has died." "It's painful to come to work now." "I hurt inside and don't even want to come here anymore." "I find myself crying and wanting to run away." "I think of any excuse not to come to work." "What's the use!" "It feels like there's been a funeral here." "I find that no one here really understands what I'm going through."

Workplace change brings about a real sense of death when employees experience a loss of co-workers, work routines, location, or control over their work. These losses are experienced with varying degrees of pain and result in a period of mourning and sometimes withdrawal.

Such behaviors as eating lunch or taking breaks alone, appearing sad, sighing, and expressing other body language that signals "Leave me alone!" are part of the depression of grief. Depressed people have less energy, and this may directly affect work output, error control, teamwork, effective communication, tardiness, and absenteeism.

Acceptance

"Now that I have been given a lemon, I'll have to make lemonade!" "Now that I have had a chance to get some of these feelings out, I can start to write that new job description." "Well, if you can't beat 'em, join 'em!" "I'm still not happy about this change, but I'm going to look at this as a challenge rather than a punishment."

Acceptance is primarily an intellectual state. If you are dying, it means that you have accepted the inevitable enough to get your financial affairs in order, complete unfinished business with loved ones, or develop a spiritual sense. You may not yet be happy with the imminent changes, but you can accommodate them.

An employee who is about to be uprooted from a familiar workplace setting and given a new job and title may reconcile the changes *intellectually* by tying up loose ends, saying good-bye to work friends, and looking at the new beginnings as a professional challenge. Still, the employee may retain negative feelings about the change. So the employee will need time to adjust *emotionally* by creating new bonds to people, places, routines, and a new identity in the reorganized workplace.

It is this emotional rebounding that brings about a more complete acceptance of the new circumstance and a completion of the grieving-healing process. When this happens, there is a balance between the head's and the heart's acceptance of workplace change.

To further expand your understanding of how people grieve, complete the following exercise on workplace change you have experienced using the Kübler-Ross descriptions of grief reactions.

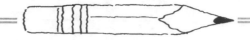

RECOGNIZING THE KÜBLER-ROSS REACTIONS

To further expand your understanding of how people grieve, complete the following exercise.

Choose the most critical workplace change-loss that you or someone you know has experienced. List your recollections about specific behaviors for each of the five Kübler-Ross categories of loss reactions.

First, briefly describe the loss situation:

_____

_____

Denial:

_____

_____

Anger:

_____

_____

Bargaining:

_____

_____

Depression:

_____

_____

Acceptance:

_____

_____

Think about how these various responses to loss are part of your own way of grieving. Also think about others you know who have similar reactions to loss. Take a few moments to jot some of these recollections down in a notebook.

The Effects of Grief on Employees

What Grieving Employees Are Feeling

Today's work environment is often characterized by swift and drastic changes. We can no longer assume that things will stay as they have been. What was once a secure "home away from home" becomes a frightening, unfriendly, and even hostile place. Seemingly nonstop workplace change can lead employees to feel anger, pain, fear, guilt, and shame. Let's look at each of these feelings in more detail and how to work through each one.

Anger

Take a rattle from a baby and there is no mistaking that angry cry. Take computer privileges away from a teenager or deny use of the family car, and be prepared for rage. Take a title, desk, parking place, job security, workplace friend, or feeling of trust away from an employee, and anger is a natural reaction.

We express anger whenever we are denied something we want, or we perceive obstacles to our goal. Have you ever gone to the copier with a rush job only to discover the machine is out of order? Or found yourself stuck in traffic with an appointment just minutes away? How many of us really enjoy having to pack up our office and move our things to a new location? Frustration converts to anger very quickly and is a natural, normal release of an inner emotional state. As many of us would say, "It's enough to make you scream!"

Anger is an expected reaction to loss and one of the natural emotions of human beings. It is never wrong to experience anger. We are not bad people when we get angry. The trouble starts when we either ignore the anger or engage in unhealthy, harmful expressions of the anger.

Unresolved anger can lead to chronic bitterness, self-hatred, grudges, and an ongoing sense of helplessness. In some cases, it can also lead to physical aches and pains, symptoms of stress, depression, and other emotional disorders. Anger that is constructively managed, however, can fuel productive change and bring about motivation to develop new skills and to complete important tasks.

Identifying Your Anger

List five things that make you angry both at work and away from work.

1. _____

2. _____

3. _____

4. _____

5. _____

Circle those that you would like to talk about with anyone at work or home. Who *can* you talk to about these feelings?

Pain

"It hurts, it hurts so much!" A young widow was sobbing, recalling the few happy years she had had with her husband who had died in an accident several weeks before. Her pain of grief—that aching feeling inside, the *emptiness* that grievers describe—is well known. But similar grieving behavior can take place in people who have been laid off from a job they loved. These people describe the same aching, empty feeling inside.

When our bonds—with people, places, routines, and even things—are broken, the physical and emotional pain of grief occurs along with anger as a part of the process. For people who have made their work and the workplace social environment the most important part of their lives, the loss or threat of loss of what has been can result in devastating pain.

As we grow and develop from infancy to adulthood, we learn who we are from important people around us—parents, brothers and sisters, other relatives, teachers, friends, colleagues, and managers. Part of our identity is tied up with our workplace role and how people around us act toward us. We read our "okay-ness" in the eyes of those important others, and when we are separated from them because of workplace change, the source of personal validation is lost—*and grieved*. The importance of workplace friends and associates takes on a greater meaning in our mobile society where, for many, co-workers are their extended family.

What Causes You Pain?

1. In what way do you see the pain of workplace change as being like the pain of a death?

   _____

   _____

   _____

2. What kind of emotional pain in another person is the most difficult for you to see?

   _____

   _____

   _____

3. What are your resources for dealing with emotional pain? Whom do you talk to?

   _____

   _____

   _____

Fear

"How will I survive this?" "What will happen to us?" "Who will take care of us?" "I'm scared, Mommy—how will we get money to live now?"

These are the words of people who have just lost a loved one, learned of a life-threatening medical diagnosis, or had their workplace drastically disrupted. Because the bottom-line issue in loss is survival, the threat or actual breaking of a bond causes fear and sometimes panic and terror. Children can be especially blunt about their fears. They often worry about economic security. When one parent dies, children express great concern for the health and well-being of the surviving parent.

Loss due to workplace change often causes employees to express similar fears about security and the future. Their families worry too. Spouses and children frequently express anxiety about how the family will live should the employee be laid off or moved to a lower-paying job with no hopes for career advancement. Conversations, both at home and at work, focus on fears, personal safety, and uncertainty about the future.

Employee fears may be specific, such as being afraid to travel, open the mail, or enter tall buildings. Employees may fear losing their health benefits or material possessions, or being unable to pay for a child's education. But there are also many general fears, such as having to face the family or friends or neighbors. Older workers may fear that they cannot learn the skills required in the new work organization.

Old childhood messages about not expressing fear may keep worries unexpressed and underground, which can lead to stress and physical and emotional problems. Many will find themselves distracted by these fears, and work performance will suffer as a result.

Uncovering Your Fears

1. What is your biggest fear about your job at this time?

   _____

   _____

   _____

2. How does this get in the way of your job performance?

   _____

   _____

   _____

3. Briefly describe how you usually handle such fears.

   _____

   _____

   _____

Guilt

"It's my fault." "I feel like I've been punished for being bad." "What did I do wrong!?" "I just wasn't good enough." "I wasn't a good enough spouse, lover, parent, son or daughter, sibling, friend, manager, co-worker, employee."

It is not uncommon for a lot of soul-searching to occur when a loved one becomes bedridden with a terminal illness or dies. Bereaved people will frequently ruminate about the many regrets they have and what they should or shouldn't have done.

Similarly, employees who are being transferred, undergoing a significant job change, or feeling in limbo between company layoffs may find many regrets surfacing about their work history. Facts often do not support any connection between an employee's performance and the reorganization or other status change. Nevertheless, many who survive a layoff—only to have their work situation profoundly altered—may blame themselves, convinced that their performance or their personality was at fault.

Getting Through Guilt

When you or someone you care about has felt guilty, what has helped the most?

_____

_____

_____

Shame

"I can't look my co-workers in the eye anymore." "Since I lost my supervisory role, I'm too embarrassed to even eat in the cafeteria." "I just know the whole neighborhood is talking about what's going on." "I can't face my parents now that I have been demoted." "I don't even tell people I meet where I work now."

Our work identity may get lost when reorganizations, mergers, and redeployments occur. If we are not on the same team anymore or not part of the decision making or have lost some of the trappings of workplace status, we feel ashamed and reluctant to let friends and neighbors know what is happening.

Shame is also a typical reaction for some types of losses, especially a loss in workplace status. It is related to the guilt feelings discussed previously in that it comes from not feeling good about ourselves or our identity now that significant changes have taken place. Shame and guilt have their roots in early childhood messages we receive and absorb—about what is good and right, about what gets us love and acceptance.

Observing Shame

Describe instances where you have observed people expressing feelings of shame in connection with transitions.

_____

_____

_____

Expressions of Grief in the Workplace

Employees who are grieving often suffer from physical symptoms, depression, anxiety, lowered morale, diminished motivation, increased stress reactions, and burnout. As the following examples illustrate, these feelings often reveal themselves in the workplace as negative thoughts and statements.

Sadness: Pain of loss, emptiness, hurt feelings. "I feel like a motherless child."

Anger: "I had something—a job description, a title, working relationships, familiar routines and procedures—and they've been taken away from me!"

"I'm mad!"

Loss of trust: "It's not fair! I did a good job for all these years, I was a loyal employee, and now look what they've done to me! I feel betrayed!"

Fear: "Am I next? What is going to happen to me? To my family? Will I survive the next reduction sweep?"

"Are we in danger, too? Could that happen here?"

Confusion: "Who am I now? How do I fit in? What am I to the organization?"

Physical aches and pains: "Ow! My back, my neck, my head, my stomach!"

What's-the-use attitude: "Why bother? This work can wait. Who cares?!"

Yearning, regret: "I wish things were back the way they were. I feel like a stepchild in a new family."

"I miss the good old days."

Return of old grief: "This reminds me of when we lost …"

Guilt: "It's my fault. If only I were better at my job or smarter."

"I should have seen the writing on the wall."

Shame: "I feel so stupid. No one in my family has ever been demoted or transferred out."

Helplessness: "I have control of nothing at work anymore!"

"I'm just a lame duck."

Marital and family distress: "My unhappiness at work has spilled over into my home life."

"We argue a lot at home now."

Changes in Employee Attitudes and Behaviors

The negative thoughts and statements that many people express while grieving often lead to changes in attitudes and behaviors. This section explains these predictable changes in conduct as they relate to the workplace.

> **Distrust:** After the shock wave of a sudden reorganization announcement and the layoffs and other changes that typically follow, employees may feel as though "the rug has been pulled out from under them." Their level of trust in the company takes a nose dive. People who feel betrayed often develop a generally suspicious, "save-your-own-skin" attitude. These suspicious employees fear for their jobs and may even withhold information from others to protect themselves.

> **Resentment:** Bitter resentment, especially toward those "above" in the organizational hierarchy, can develop as the workplace that had been known and secure becomes cold, frightening, and uncertain. Many people have a need to blame someone and a desire to "get even." This can result in work slowdown, lack of teamwork or follow-up, and even hostile, destructive behaviors.

> **Apathy:** Seeing hard-working, dedicated employees get laid off undermines co-workers' own motivation to produce. Not knowing what the future holds makes many people feel in limbo, and their apathy produces absenteeism, overlong breaks, and inefficiency. Some can be heard saying, "What's the use of working hard?—it doesn't pay!"

> **Desperation:** Many employees respond to change or the threat of change with nervousness, hyperactivity, and undue worry about pleasing the boss. They say to themselves, "If I get more paperwork out, start the day earlier and stay later, and come in on weekends, maybe I'll get to stay or keep my staff or this office." Stress and its negative effects usually accompany this behavior.

> **Play It Safe:** When employees are constantly waiting for the ax to fall, they fear taking risks and set easily reached work goals to avoid a poor evaluation. Goals are set low, creative approaches to problem solving are scarce, and no one wants to take any chance of looking bad. While things are in a freeze, so is productivity. For many, there is a fear of complaining about how difficult things are, and this unexpressed fear can fester.

> **Helplessness:** During transition, many employees express a sense of helplessness and feeling overwhelmed. "I'll never be able to get the job done." "There is no support and I have to do it all by myself." "I'm afraid to ask my supervisor for help." Many people experience a sinking feeling of low self-confidence, and this contributes to apathy or bitterness and even rage.

Grief Reactions to Change-Loss

The table below summarizes feelings, attitudes, and behaviors that are grief reactions to loss in the workplace, and it illustrates the connections among them. Take a few minutes to look over these three categories of reactions. Think about any workplace change-loss that you or someone you know has experienced. Then circle any items in the Attitudes and Behaviors columns that you or the other person has experienced.

Feelings	Attitudes	Behaviors
Anger	"Oh, yeah?!" Resentment Bitterness "The hell with it!" "I'll get even." Can't be bothered Look out for No. 1	Hostile acts Lowered productivity Destructiveness Stealing Work left undone Errors Sarcastic joking
Pain	"What's the use?!" "Nothing matters. "Why bother?"	Withdrawal Isolation Low efficiency Low energy Errors
Fear	"Don't stick your neck out." "Play it safe." Apathy	Rigidity Lack of creativity, boredom Tentative action Errors Holding on to staff, resources
Guilt	Self-consciousness "I've been bad." Negative self-concept "I should have been the one let go."	Hiding Nervousness Errors
Shame	"I'm not good enough." "They don't like me." "I want to run away."	Hiding Avoidance Isolation Errors

Why Productivity Plummets Amid Grief

When employees are expressing the feelings, attitudes, and behaviors that are normal reactions to grief, productivity tends to plummet. The preceding table on Grief Reactions to Change-Loss helps you to see why. The reasons can be summarized as follows:

➢ **Loss of Loyalty:** Grieving people, who are hurt and bitter and have no sense of security, experience a significant drop in loyalty to company goals.

➢ **Revenge:** Many say they will seek revenge in any way possible. Others simply go through the motions to get through another day and put out little real effort. For still others, anger influences the work pace and causes missed deadlines, lost contracts, theft, and sabotaged projects.

➢ **Accidents and Errors:** Some people become so frantic that they are prone to accidents and errors that might not normally occur.

➢ **Low Morale:** The lowered morale of employees who feel unfairly treated or are embittered by friends' layoffs drains energy from the work force. These employees may also be distracted by worry about losses still to come, in the same way they would be distracted if they were worried about critical illness in their family.

➢ **Avoiding Work:** Many employees begin to dread coming to work. There is increased tardiness, absenteeism, and medical complaints. Drug and alcohol abuse may also increase as employees self-medicate to cope with the constant workplace agitation and related home conflicts.

➢ **Holding Back:** To minimize risk of failure, managers may set easily attainable goals.

➢ **Stress:** The *threat* of loss and the grief over what has already been lost increases stress levels. The ongoing stress of unattended grief has psychological as well as physical repercussions. As a result, productivity is lowered in both hidden and obvious ways.

Effects on Productivity

1. Which of the above have you observed when change has occurred in your workplace?

   _____

   _____

   _____

2. List any additional hidden or obvious reasons for lowered productivity during workplace change that you may be aware of.

   _____

   _____

   _____

The Pitfalls of Not Attending to Grief

As we move through life, unfinished loss material may be stored within us, depending on how much we learned to *express* feelings rather than "stuff" them. Think about it. How willing are we to share with our co-workers how we feel—or to hear how they really feel? Every day we ask one another questions such as "How are you?" "How's it going?" "What's up today?" But are we really receptive to hearing that someone is angry, hurting, or scared? We cannot deny that feelings exist, yet our society expects us to keep our feelings to ourselves.

Childhood Messages Influence Current Expression

Very early in life we learn through statements such as the following when it is okay and not okay to express fear, sadness, and other feelings:

➤ *"Don't raise your voice!"*

➤ *"Cry baby!"*

➤ *"Keep crying and I'll give you something to really cry about!"*

➤ *"Don't be a baby, there's nothing to be afraid of."*

Early childhood messages such as these influence how we express feelings in later life. When we get the message that feelings are *not okay*, we tend to hold them in or suppress them. Then when a life change or loss occurs and the normal reaction would be to express appropriate anger, sadness, or fear, we may "stuff it."

This allows the anger, sadness, and fear to accumulate. It is this accumulated, unresolved loss material that comes to the surface and causes difficulty when there is a new loss.

To help you to more fully understand the influence of childhood messages on current grief, complete the exercise on the next page.

WAS/IS IT OKAY TO EXPRESS YOUR FEELINGS?

From childhood messages that we receive from parents or other important grownups, we learn whether it is okay to say how we feel, or even if it is okay to feel emotions at all. Many of us as children perceive that it is *not* okay or safe to express how we feel. As a result, in later life situations, such as workplace change or other loss, we do not express the anger, hurt, and fear that are normal reactions. We stuff it down instead.

This exercise focuses on three important grief feelings—anger, sadness, and fear. Imagine yourself back in your childhood. See how much you can recall of your early childhood messages from parents or other adults about feelings. Was it okay to be angry, to cry, or to be afraid?

1. Under the Childhood Messages column, briefly state what you recall hearing as a child about each of the feelings—anger, sadness/crying, and fear.

2. Rate how much you still behave according to the old messages.

Feelings	Childhood Messages	Current Rating (How much message is still in effect?)
Anger	_____ _____	10 9 8 7 6 5 4 3 2 1
Sadness/crying	_____ _____	10 9 8 7 6 5 4 3 2 1
Fear	_____ _____	10 9 8 7 6 5 4 3 2 1

Completing this exercise will help you gauge how aware you are of the current effect of the old messages. Even messages you cannot recall can influence you. Losses you were not allowed to grieve are stored internally, and over the years, the "pot" of unfinished business fills up.

The Three Sources of Unresolved Grief

Storing away, rather than addressing, grief can have an intensely negative effect on how we perceive new losses. So it is helpful to look at the three sources of unresolved grief. These are explained with The Unfinished Business Model, below.

Developmental Loss

Developmental Loss

First, we store up loss material from the natural and expected changes that occur throughout our normal development: starting school, getting a new brother or sister, leaving home, our first job, changing jobs. Each time there is a change or transition that is a normal part of life, we lose what was before. If we are never given the opportunity to express any feelings about these changes, we store the feelings.

Breaking of Actual Bonds

Second, we store up loss material when bonds we have made are broken, such as when a loved one moves away, a pet dies, a beloved toy is lost, a friend rejects us, we are dropped from a team, or we lose a job, miss the promotion, or are moved to another work team in a new location. As described earlier, whenever an attachment bond is broken, there is grief, and grief wants to cry and rage. If we have been denied the right to externalize or get these feelings out, we store them away.

Threat of Loss

Third, we store up loss material when we live under constant threat of loss, whether it stems from chronic financial insecurity, an abusive family life, low self-esteem, a gravely ill family member, or an unsafe living environment. Because this threat of loss of someone or something is ongoing, it creates a highly destructive and painful collection of unfinished business that gets stored up if it is not managed well. This scenario is also true for people who experience constant anxiety, stress, and grief as a result of earlier trauma.

The Costs of Storing, Rather Than Addressing, Grief

The feelings of hurt, anger, and fear and the attitudes and behaviors of the grief reaction are normal and expected human responses to loss. But many people are uncomfortable addressing their grief reactions—or they have perceived from their family and workplace that outward expressions of grief are not okay. Storing away this unfinished business, however, takes its toll on a person physically and emotionally in lost energy, overreactions, and chronic stress, as explained below.

> ### Energy Cost

We pay a price in energy consumed each time we stuff old grief, anger, fear, shame, and guilt into that internal storage bin. The energy used to keep the lid on this bin of unfinished grief is thus unavailable for other, more productive purposes in our lives—solving problems, loving, being creative, or working. The more unfinished business we store, the more energy is needed to hold the lid down on the accumulated stuff, often resulting in fatigue, inefficiency, and lowered motivation.

> ### Overreaction

Accumulated unfinished business filters into every aspect of our behavior. Doctors and nurses bring their unfinished business to the bedside of every patient. Corporate managers carry their unfinished business into each decision they make. Employees faced with current grief due to workplace change, loss, and trauma also carry the echoes of old unfinished grief into their daily lives. The old, stored feelings mingle with the new grief. Even worse, we often are not aware that this is happening. When the pool of stored negativity is too full, even a small crisis can result in an overreaction. The lid blows off the storage bin and causes a more severe grief reaction.

> ### Chronic Stress Reaction

Keeping the old loss material under wraps increases the risk for physical and emotional symptoms, as well as for burnout and an inability to work through the grieving-healing process.

When grief is unattended, the stress, energy drain, extreme fatigue, and negative attitudes have a direct effect on employee productivity. This is why it is so important to help employees cope with the loss, trauma, and grief that come from workplace change.

New Meanings for the New Workplace

Whenever there is change, there are endings. Someone or something has been left behind. We not only relinquish one world but find ourselves in a new world and must redefine who we now are (Niemeyer, 2001).

"Who am I now?" asks the grieving widow. "What is expected of me in this reorganized company?" asks the worker in a recently acquired corporation. "I just can't get my bearings." "I'll never learn this new software program." "I don't know who I am in this place anymore." People who have had a significant change in their work environment or private lives typically make these statements. They find themselves in a strange, new world.

As employees move through grief, they must find new meanings of who they are now and how they will live and work in their new world. The picture of themselves—as a spouse, a manager, or the acknowledged "expert" in the former world—no longer fits the new situation. People experiencing change must rewrite the script of their lives and in some way reinvent who they are now vs. then.

Employees who have survived changes must go through a period of grieving, establishing new meanings and creating new attachments, to successfully adjust and become productive in the new work world. Organizations that recognize this and provide the understanding and support employees need have the greatest likelihood of realizing their financial objectives.

P A R T 4

Helping

Employees Cope

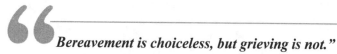

Today's leaders have to know how to accomplish individual and organizational transitions."

–**David M. Noer,** *Healing the Wounds*

Bereavement is choiceless, but grieving is not."

–**Thomas Attig,** *How We Grieve*

Workplace Change and Loss:
The Burdens and Benefits

If you go through the tumbler of life, you can come out crushed or polished."

–Elisabeth Kübler-Ross, M.D.,
Living With Death and Dying

As we travel through life and experience its expected and unexpected twists and turns, we may look back at the journey and see that crisis and loss have pushed us in new directions, and that these have been directions that resulted in some good. It is possible to acknowledge "the gift of loss."

This does not mean that we wanted the loss to occur or that we would still not want to recover whatever was lost—a person, good job, or career dream. Yet we are able to acknowledge that the loss has happened and that by grieving the loss we were able to move on to other pathways that eventually led to healing, growth, and joy.

So, too, can we consider traumatic workplace changes, loss, and grief as detours in life's roadway, leading us to new skills, new work, a new career, and the possibilities for renewed joy and satisfaction in life.

Understanding the natural and expected flow of human reactions as employees move from the old to the new enables managers to intervene with clarity and compassion. People undergoing change need to experience a transition time between who they were and who and what they will be. When appropriate programs are instituted, organizations in transition will have the greatest potential for realizing the business objectives that are driving the changes.

This is a stormy period lacking familiar routines, feelings, and thoughts. People who are in the grief process need special attention. As individuals, we can offer our attention and assistance to colleagues because we are a friend or because it is a responsibility of our work role. In this part, you will learn how to help others and how organizations can create programs to support the grieving process during and after planned and unexpected change.

The Four Tasks of Workplace Mourning

The grief reaction is a psychological trauma just as a wound or a burn is a physical trauma. The human grief response is an attempt to reestablish the individual's emotional balance in the same way that physical healing reestablishes the body's well-being. For individuals to recover their equilibrium, a period of grieving behavior is necessary.

To complete the grieving process, the person must address each of the *Four Tasks of Mourning*, as described by Harvard psychologist Dr. J. William Worden. Modified for application to the work setting, the four tasks of workplace mourning are:

> **Task 1: Accepting the Reality of the Change-Loss**
>
> **Task 2: Addressing the Pain and Other Feelings of Grief**
>
> **Task 3: Making the Needed Changes for a New Work Situation**
>
> **Task 4: Developing a New Group Identity and Making New Bonds**

If employees do not sufficiently address these tasks, their mourning will be incomplete, and they will store unfinished loss pain (Worden, 1991). Let's examine these tasks individually and how you can help employees with each one.

Task 1: Accepting the Reality of the Loss

For employees to let go of "how it used to be," they must acknowledge the loss. An individual must face the reality that something has ended and things will never be the same. People may attempt to avoid and deny that a change has occurred or is about to. They may resist acknowledging the "endings" as well as the new personnel who represent "new beginnings."

For example, a young child who knows a new baby is coming into the family may not want to think about it and may have bad dreams or may even fantasize about ways to prevent it from happening. Once the new baby is home, however, the child must face the reality that the family organization is forever altered and the child's place in the family—as the only child—is gone forever. The child may cry, act helpless, and demand attention as though still the only child. In these ways the child resists the reality of the end of "what was."

Many employees "don't think about" the changes in store for them—and when the change actually occurs, they feel as if they were taken by surprise.

Denying the reality of the loss can also take the form of ignoring the significance of the loss. Many people say things such as: "No problem!" "I wasn't so crazy about that old job anyway." "Those people in my old office weren't so wonderful after all." People can go in and out of believing and denying that the change has taken place or is about to take place.

> ### Case: Head/Heart Split
>
> A man sits at his desk, his head in his hands, quietly fighting back tears. He has been reassigned to another office in his division. He is in pain because he is being separated from work friends who have become a support for him over the years and who have accepted him for who he is. Then he sits up and wipes his face and says, "It's probably a good thing that I'm being transferred." He admits that it may actually be better for his career. He mentions several other benefits of the change—and then the tears begin to well up in his eyes again.
>
> His intellect or "head" has accepted the reality, but his emotional self or "heart" has not. We call this the *Head/Heart Split*. People often find it easier to let go of their former work situation with their heads even as they continue to hold on with their hearts.

How to Help with Task 1: Accepting the Reality of the Loss

1. Talk about what is being lost as a result of the change. Employees who are unable to openly acknowledge that the change has happened or is about to happen need help to do so. Encourage them to say out loud what is being lost as a result of the workplace change and how these losses are affecting them. In this way, the reality of the situation will be more likely to surface.

2. Spend time talking with individual employees about the value of their former work setting and honor the contributions made to staff and to the company. This helps to place what used to be in the past.

3. Use a good-bye ritual. This can be very helpful, especially when employees are changing locations. It can be done informally, by looking at the area and saying "good-bye" (verbally or non-verbally) to whatever was special about the space or by writing the good-byes on paper. Encourage employees to take photos of the old space and put them up in the new location.

4. Create a memory book or memory letter and share it at a group meeting.

5. Take familiar objects—wall hangings, desk accessories, a piece of carpet—from the old setting to the new location and place them in symbolic spots.

6. Take employees to visit the new staff and location. If possible, have them visit the new setting before they officially begin work.

Task 2: Addressing the Pain and Other Feelings of Grief

The pain of grief is physical as well as emotional. That is why people who have experienced loss will often say, "I feel as though I have been punched in the stomach." A loss of any type can bring about those hurting, aching, empty feelings.

It is important that people not ignore these feelings but tell someone about them as well. It is also important for people assisting those who are grieving to be accepting of that pain. People whose grieving is not accepted can find themselves stuck in grief for years.

The pain of others can be hard to take. Even those whose job it is to help people through loss often find it difficult to listen as someone starts to worry, cry, or rage about changes in their work role.

But changing the subject or inventing distractions is not a productive way of dealing with the grieving-healing process. Although many of us think of tears as a sign of weakness, or anger as lack of control, or worrying as a lack of courage, we must recognize that these *sounds of grief are sounds of healing.*

How to Help with Task 2: Addressing the Pain and Other Feelings of Grief

Completing this task requires an employee to express the feelings and pain of grief. Having an *effective listener* is very important.

1. Listen! Listen! Listen! Spend time, take a walk together, have lunch. Let people know their feelings are *normal*. Postpone your own agenda and attend to theirs.

2. Offer specific help with some of their work, if possible.

3. Help them seek professional help if things get out of control.

4. Encourage them to keep a journal of feelings and thoughts about the change-loss.

5. Avoid giving advice and refrain from sharing your own experiences with grief until after they have expressed their feelings. People who are grieving appreciate knowing that others have gone through what they are going through but only after they have had the room to express themselves.

6. Refrain from offering distractions such as telling jokes or changing the subject.

7. Avoid setting deadlines for "getting over this."

Task 3: Making the Needed Changes for a New Work Situation

This task is designed to help employees adjust to the new workplace and requires that they face the workday with many details of change:

> ➤ Adjust to a new space with new people. Without their old social network, they soon become aware of just how important the "old gang" was in making the workday pleasant and quick. They probably miss the reliable colleague who was always available to answer questions.

> ➤ Rely on untried or rusty skills.

> ➤ Familiarize themselves with a new location for supplies.

> ➤ Learn how to use new work equipment, routines, and schedules.

> ➤ Adjust to new commuting and parking arrangements, lunch facilities, dress codes, or other new "norms."

Perhaps the most significant concern many employees will have is "How do I fit in here?" They will begin to question their new role in the organizational structure. People worry about their previous group identity and the formation of a new one almost as soon as a change is announced or the rumors start flying.

They may resent having to develop new skills and to prove themselves to others once again. Some will be fearful that they will not get along with new co-workers. Others may be irritated at not having the same support services as in the former workplace setting. People report that they find themselves feeling less in control, helpless, and inadequate. This, in turn, can trigger old childhood feelings of being "not good enough" or "not lovable."

The ongoing waves of change cause many a frustrated employee to say, "Just when I thought everything was settled, we've got another new change to deal with!"

Employees who do not adequately address Task 3 may resist learning new skills and remain in a state of helplessness, requiring much assistance and supervision. Or they may isolate themselves from the work group whenever possible. Much of the resistance to a new work environment is a result of the employee's not accepting that the change is permanent.

The work of Task 3 is a critical turning point for completing the grieving-healing process. People who do not address this task will feel as if their grief is never resolved. Instead, it will be stored, leaving both the employee and management unhappy. Successful change management requires that employees fully address the loss of what was before they can completely adopt and experience the merits of what will be.

How to Help with Task 3: Making the Needed Changes for a New Work Situation

1. Supply information about the new work situation to the employee as soon as possible.

2. Identify the new skills and knowledge needed to get the job done.

3. Locate training for new skills (both in-house training programs and those outside of the workplace).

4. Help with new location arrangements—setting up equipment, arranging desks, finding storage space.

5. Help employees see the move or change as part of their larger career picture.

Task 4: Developing a New Group Identity and Making New Bonds

A newly transferred employee may continue to maintain ties with work friends in the former organization. The bonds are typically not severed in one quick cut. Detaching from the people, surroundings, and routines of the former work situation takes time, but eventually the individual will look to the new work arrangement as the workplace home.

Visits to the former group and phone calls to former colleagues will begin to diminish. Friendship and support needs will increasingly be filled by the new colleagues. Relocated employees will spend less time thinking about what was and more time thinking about what is now and what are the possibilities for the future.

Specifically, employees begin to:

➤ Invest energy from former workplace connections into the creation of new bonds

➤ Spend less time on memories of the past and have less intense feelings of grief

➤ Recognize the value of their role in the new situation, while appreciating the value of the former work group

➤ Find that yearning for the former work setting interferes less and less in their new work tasks. They can now say to themselves, "I know who I am and how I fit in to this new work situation."

An employee who insists that "I can't let go" of what was, and who resists bonding with the new work situation is not addressing Task 4. This indicates difficulty in adjusting to the new organization. Personal traits, unfinished loss material, poor transition management, and lack of organization in the new work setting can all contribute to an employee's inability to accomplish Task 4.

How to Help with Task 4: Developing a New Group Identity and Making New Bonds

1. Provide orientation to the new work situation.

2. Create informal social contacts with others in the new situation.

3. Organize team-building activities with the new work group by including them in project teams, committees, and process-improvement teams.

4. Assist employees with meeting their personal adjustment needs in the new situation—facilities, resources, comfort.

5. Provide opportunities to talk about the former workplace and "how we did things then."

6. Acknowledge the value of former experiences and relationships.

7. Create new rituals and traditions, such as welcoming ceremonies and other forms of personal recognition.

WORKING THROUGH GRIEVING TO HEALING

Choose one workplace change you have experienced. For each of the four tasks, indicate how much still must be done to reach a degree of completion. Circle the responses (a, b, c, or d) that best describe your current feelings.

_____
_____
_____
_____

Briefly describe the workplace change:

_____
_____
_____
_____

Task 1: Accepting the Reality of the Loss

a. Pretty much believe it now.

b. Going in and out of believing it happened.

c. Still have a lot to do. Still can't believe it happened.

d. Other: _____

_____

Task 2: Reaching the Pain and Other Feelings of Grief

a. A lot of painful feelings have come up about this change.

b. Some painful feelings came up about this change.

c. Very few feelings came up about this change.

d. Other: _____

_____

CONTINUED

CONTINUED

Task 3: Make the Needed Changes for a New Work Situation

   a. I've done what I need to do—learned new skills, adjusted to new routines, created new work schedules for the new situation.

   b. I'm still working on getting the new skills and understanding the new routines.

   c. I haven't yet been able to adjust to the new work situation.

   d. Other _____

   _____

   _____

Task 4: Develop a New Group Identity and Make New Bonds

   a. I really feel that I fit in with the new group.

   b. Most of the time I feel that I fit in with the new group.

   c. I'm still working on fitting in with the new folks.

   d. Other _____

   _____

   _____

Where you have circled *b* or *c* above, choose and list below items from the "How to Help" sections of the Four Tasks presented previously, which may help you in further addressing each task.

_____

_____

_____

The four tasks of the grieving-healing process set forth the work that must be done to complete grieving and reach a state of healing and growth. There are specific ways to facilitate accomplishing each task.

Helping People Heal by Listening

Much of the help we give to others in accomplishing the tasks of mourning requires that we be truly available to hear and respond to what they say. To be an active listener:

> Avoid giving advice or trying to cut off grief

> Keep your attention focused on what the other person is saying; defer to his or her agenda

> Avoid asking questions that begin with "Why…"

Remember: You cannot fix grief! But you can listen to a person who is grieving. Listeners who realize that the expression of feelings is a normal, healthy response to grief, and thus are comfortable with the grieving, can be of tremendous help. A grieving, traumatized person needs to be heard—really heard.

When you listen in a passive, disinterested way, the grieving person may perceive that you are wondering, "When will this be over?" You may fail to make eye contact, become easily distracted, and frequently change the subject from the grief. The grieving person will quickly become aware of your lack of interest and will usually terminate the conversation and avoid you in the future.

Five Steps to Helpful Listening

Helpful listening is done in an active way. This signals the grieving person that the listener is ready and willing to hear. The five steps to helpful listening do not have to take place in sequence. They can flow together or can occur in combination and build on each other.

Step 1: Show interest non-verbally

Face the speaker, make eye contact, nod, and use expressions and body language to indicate "I hear you." Be careful not to indicate judgment by such facial and body expressions as raising an eyebrow, shrugging, or turning away from the speaker.

Step 2: Show interest orally

Use affirming sounds or words such as "Uh huh," "Mm hmm," and "I hear you." As in Step 1, assume a nonjudgmental and receptive attitude. Avoid comments that block the flow of expression from the grieving person, such as "I hate to hear that!" "Don't tell me that." "I know exactly how you feel." If you feel sorrow, however, it is acceptable to let tears come. This is a time to say, "I'm sad too."

Step 3: Open the conversational door

So far, you have been active in attending to the speaker through non-verbal behavior and brief sounds or phrases that affirm your willingness to hear the speaker. You can now increase your participation by using statements that clearly encourage the grieving person. Statements such as "Yes, go on," "Tell me more," and "I'd like to hear more about that" will directly invite the grieving person to talk more about a particular issue.

Step 4: Rephrase the speaker's content

Listen for meaning! In this step, say back to the speaker, in your own words, the essential meaning of what you heard. This is called *paraphrasing*. Here are a few examples:

"So you have given up making any career plans since the downsizing started."

"It sounds like you don't even want to come to work anymore."

"Sounds like you can't get those terrible pictures out of you mind."

Paraphrasing has three advantages:

➤ It lets the grieving person know that he really has your full attention

➤ It provides an accuracy check on what you believe was said

➤ It tells the speaker she has been understood

This is not the time to give advice or talk about your own worries. Instead, pay attention to and respect the speaker's agenda. Employees who feel understood will feel less isolated and better able to continue dealing with their own painful reactions.

Step 5: Say what you hear the speaker feeling

Listen for feeling! The goal in this step is simply to tell the speaker what you believe he or she is feeling. This assures the grieving person that he is being understood at the emotional level.

As a *helping listener* you will determine how the grieving person feels by what has been said and by what has been communicated through facial expression and body language. Of course the content of what is being said will provide clues to how the speaker is feeling, but so will the tone of voice; slowness or rapidity of speech; a sad, angry, or frightened face; tears and words of anger or cursing; hand and arm gestures; body slouching; and shaking of the head. Listen for the emotional music behind the words.

For example, you can say:

"You're really angry about how you were told about the transfer."

"You seem frightened about what is going to happen to your job."

"This has been a very upsetting time for you."

"You're worried about how you will fit into the new organization."

Using words such as "upset," "angry" or "hurt" will let the grieving person know that you recognize how she feels. Being understood in this way allows grieving people to release their pain and other emotional energy, helping them to move along in the grieving process toward healing.

Practice the five active listening skills on friends and family and notice the different way they begin to respond to you. Work on the first three steps for a week or two, and then start to use the paraphrasing and feeling-response techniques of Steps 4 and 5.

People generally appreciate being heard and feeling understood. Individuals dealing with grief are in great need of this kind of helpful listening.

Now try the following Helpful Listening exercise, and check your answers with the recommended responses in the Appendix.

HELPFUL LISTENING

Following are three statements you might hear from a person dealing with transition grief. For each statement, write a response that communicates to the grieving person that you know the feelings she is having. There can be more than one good response to each item.

For example:

Grieving person: *"I don't know what I'll do if they cut my hours."*
Helping listener: *"You're pretty worried about that."*

Grieving person: *"I hate the way they 'retired' Mary and Jack."*
Helpful listener: *"That made you pretty angry."*

1. Grieving Employee: *"I hate the way they just don't tell you anything."*

   Your helpful listening response:

   _____

2. Grieving Employee: *"It's so gloomy and empty in here now that the transfers have gone through."*

   Your helpful listening response:

   _____

3. Grieving Employee: *"Now that we have been reorganized, I don't know what will happen to my career."*

   Your helpful listening response:

   _____

4. Grieving employee: *"I can't get rid of the feeling of doom here now."*

   Your helpful listening response:

   _____

Compare your answers with the author's suggestions in the Appendix.

Do's and Don'ts for Supporting Grieving Employees

In general, you can be best equipped to help employees through workplace change-loss grief if you:

➤ Accept their feelings without judgment

➤ Are aware of your own upset feelings

➤ Are prepared for the grieving person's anger

➤ Know when to suggest more specialized help

With this general advice in mind, there are many specific suggestions you can apply when offering support to a grieving employee—things you should do and things you should avoid, as you will see in the following do's and don'ts.

Do:

➤ **Put your own loss material aside for the moment.** If your own grief comes up while helping someone who is grieving, make a mental note to talk to a friend about it later—and be sure to do so. It is difficult to help anyone when your own unfinished business keeps surfacing.

➤ **Be okay with silence**—it can be golden for a person in pain. Just stay with the person.

➤ **Let the speaker know it is okay to express feelings,** to cry, or to say what is in his or her heart.

➤ **Honor confidentiality.** Do not repeat to others what has been shared with you.

➤ **Keep your commitments.** If you say, "Let's have lunch and talk," be sure you follow up.

➤ **Allow enough time** to be with the grieving person. Do not start a conversation when you have another commitment in a few minutes.

➤ **Be alert to signs of trouble.** Some employees may be experiencing multiple losses, problems at home, or medical conditions, or they may have personalities that make them especially vulnerable to workplace change. Additionally, employees who have experienced a disaster or trauma may suffer post-traumatic stress reactions. Behavioral signs of trouble include:

- Extreme changes in behavior
- Talk of suicide or idle threats of homicide
- Flashbacks
- Lack of appetite
- Insomnia or nightmares
- Prolonged fatigue
- Severe numbness
- Disorientation
- Continued memory loss
- Inability to concentrate
- Absenteeism
- Workaholism
- Abuse of drugs or alcohol
- Extreme withdrawal
- Extreme hyperactivity
- Unusual irritability
- Many physical complaints

➤ **Refer employees with extreme behaviors** that last beyond a few weeks to employee assistance counselors, human resources, the company nurse, or a medical or mental health professional.

Don't:

> ➤ **Ask too many questions.** Questions can stop the flow of an employee's expression of feelings.

> ➤ **Speak in platitudes** such as "Everything will work out" or "This is the Creator's will." People who are hurting may not be able to accept this. What they need most at first is to be heard—without judgment.

> ➤ **Try to minimize feelings.** Never say "You really shouldn't feel that way" or "Now, now, it's really not that bad" or "You're lucky you still have a job."

> ➤ **Take personally any anger** directed at you. Grief-reaction anger frequently spills over onto people who do not deserve it. This will diminish as individuals vent their feelings. Remember, you are not the object of their anger. Use the five helpful listening skills and repeat back to them that you see how angry and upset they are. This acknowledgment usually helps angry people hear their own rage.

> ➤ **Make the mistake of believing, incorrectly, that you, as an organizational leader, are exempt from grief reactions** and must put on a strong, unemotional face. You may fool the people around you, but you will not fool your own body and mind. By acknowledging your own grief material, old and new, and talking with someone else about it, you will increase your ability to help other employees, and your organization will benefit.

Quick Tips for Helping

Two common shortcomings in dealing with people in grief are doing too little—glossing over what has happened—or doing too much, such as offering inappropriate "comfort" and advice. Here are some quick tips for striking just the right balance.

➤ Listen to the person! Avoid giving advice or saying "What you should do is…"

➤ Stay connected. Make contact; do not avoid grieving individuals.

➤ Talk about whatever is brought up. Follow *their* agenda.

➤ Ask about feelings, as in: "What concerns you most about the reorganization?"

➤ Avoid trading war stories too soon. After employees have had time to talk and grieve, they will probably welcome hearing about your change-loss experience—but not before.

➤ Remain nonjudgmental in the face of strong emotion. Keep in mind that the angry feelings belong to the other person.

➤ Help start the change process in small ways. Offer to help with the physical move, compile a new directory of company names and resources, obtain new organizational charts, or review or help employees create new performance objectives.

➤ Help people keep part of the old system as they enter the new place. Save some visual symbol, such as an old logo or photos.

➤ Help break the ice with new staff. Arrange for employees to have lunch with one or two new team members.

➤ Share information about the new system. Tell employees anything you know about the new management that is hopeful and supportive.

Helping a Co-Worker Through Grief

Think of a person you know who is dealing with workplace grief. To be of help to that person, which of the preceding tips for helping would you plan to use? List them in the spaces below.

Plans for assisting a grieving employee:

1. _____
   _____
   _____

2. _____
   _____
   _____

3. _____
   _____
   _____

4. _____
   _____
   _____

5. _____
   _____
   _____

Ten Guidelines for Organizations Undergoing Change

Organizations in transition typically encounter similar problems, but applying the 10 guidelines that follow will help prevent these problems from happening. The comments that follow each problem below indicate how others have implemented the guideline and provide suggestions that may work in your organization.

1. **Provide a continuous flow of accurate and up-to-date information about the coming change throughout the entire process.**

   Problem: A lack of accurate, current, and official information powers the rumor mills, causing employees needless anxiety and pain. They lose trust in the company. Without word from an authorized spokesperson, employees focus on their own fantasies of what they think will happen, which can lead to needless grieving.

   Comment: One senior director of a government agency undergoing reorganization and requiring massive redeployment set up monthly "town meetings" to keep 1,100 employees informed of developments. Other organizations use memos, e-mail, and unit meetings to keep valid information flowing and to squelch rumors. Human resources professionals note that a lack of information creates a climate of uncertainty, which feeds employee distrust.

2. **Maintain a knowledge base about predictable reactions of change-loss grief and the skills for responding to people who are mourning.**

   Problem: If you do not know what to expect from a grieving person, the feelings can be upsetting to you.

   Comment: The more you can anticipate feelings, attitudes, and behaviors caused by grief, the more comfortable you will be talking to a grieving employee. And having helpful listening and response skills, as well as specific helping techniques, will reduce your own stress.

   Managers, human resources specialists, organizational development consultants, employee assistance staff, industrial health nurses, and consulting mental health professionals are all in a position to help employees cope with grief. So are the co-workers of grieving employees. Organizations that train staff identified to assist employees through grief will increase their chances for realizing post-transition business objectives.

3. **Remain aware of your own loss and grief issues that may be activated by the change-loss or traumatic event.**

   Problem: Managers often struggle with their own loss issues in times of change. Failure to acknowledge this in some way makes you more anxious and less available to others.

Comment: All persons in the midst of a corporate transition, regardless of their roles, are subject to grief reactions. If you have unfinished grief issues, talk with a close work friend, a consultant, or someone outside the organization. Writing down your feelings and concerns in a private journal can help to relieve grief. Externalizing your grief in these ways relieves the pressure and enables you to more effectively help others.

4. **Be aware of the realities of the specific change-loss events and their effects on all employees.**

   Problem: When managers avoid acknowledging the effects of workplace changes on employees, they cannot plan for employee support. Managers who are in denial about the coming changes in their organization may also be in denial about the reactions of their employees.

   Comment: Denial of impending loss and of the potential effects on the workforce is not unusual for some managers and organization executives. Being out of touch with how employees are reacting can lead to a serious breakdown in morale and fallen productivity.

   One division director arranged for more than 1,000 employees to have direct access to him via confidential, anonymous e-mail. Each day he read what employees were concerned about and responded to the messages on a computer bulletin board. The trust level remained high and the level of transition grief was significantly diminished.

5. **Acknowledge the value and contributions of the previous workplace situation.**

   Problem: When employees feel that their former organizational unit or group has been attacked or the value of its contributions discounted, they are typically angry, defensive, and resentful of the new organizational regime.

   Comment: Rituals and ceremonies, even letters acknowledging the value and contribution of the old group, will facilitate letting go of the past and accepting the new beginnings.

6. **Provide for continuity between the former workplace and the new by creating transitional roles, reporting relationships, and organizational groupings. Generate informal and formal organizational events to help people feel that they are still a valued part of the organization.**

   Problem: Employees are most likely to feel confused and anxious during the unstable transition period.

   Comment: Provide temporary titles, appoint transition teams with specific tasks, and give frequent informational updates as the transition moves along. This creates a sense of structure and stability for employees as well as a feeling of involvement, control, and participation in the process.

7. **Provide opportunities for people to grieve by providing "ending" rituals for the former situation as well as formal and informal grief support services.**

   Problem: When employees have no opportunities to express their grief, those feelings are stuffed or go underground. Without a means of channeling their fears and other concerns, they have no internal support system with which to address the Four Tasks of Mourning. As a result, they get "stuck in grief."

   Comment: People who are upset and grieving need to be heard. When they are free to express their concerns, they are addressing the second of Worden's Four Tasks of Mourning. One executive regularly scheduled roundtable meetings during which small groups of employees could express grief and ask questions. Others have hired outside grief consultants to facilitate groups.

   An ending ritual, at which an entire department or group says good-bye to "the way we were" also helps with letting go. For example, employees can create a formal history of the group or department or unit. They can also assemble a memory book of symbolic photos to be displayed at an ending or good-bye ceremony. Planting a tree or putting up a plaque in honor of the old group can also help employees to let go of the past and look to the future.

   Hold meetings for explaining how change in the workplace brings about grief in the workplace and what people can expect from grief reactions. Providing weekly support groups and offering individual counseling can also be important contributions to supporting employees through the grieving-healing process.

8. **Offer opportunities for people to discover, as soon as possible, the part they will play in the new work organization.**

   Problem: Not knowing their planned future role poses a major threat to employees facing workplace change. This breeds anxiety. The employees' personal work identity and social network developed in the former group may not be transferable to the new group. They are uncertain about their new titles or how well they will be accepted or will perform in the new workplace.

   Comment: As soon as possible, give employees an opportunity to learn about the new system. Orient them to the new location, equipment, other staff, schedules, and procedures to give them a sense of the new work environment. Where new skills are required for new job descriptions, provide training as soon as possible. Knowing what is expected will reduce employee anxiety and establish clear work goals. For many, these specific objectives may help them to reestablish career goals. The loss of dreams and hopes as a result of workplace change can be as hurtful as more concrete losses.

9. **Recognize that many employees will be, at best, ambivalent about and possibly resentful of the new arrangements and will require time to complete the tasks of the mourning-healing process.**

Problem: Impatience with the time it takes employees "to get over it" and "get up to speed" can slow their movement through the grief process.

Comment: Everyone grieves differently and has a different grief time frame. Try to determine where each employee is in the Four Tasks of Mourning. This way, you can help individuals more effectively. Some employees will require extra time to gradually reenter the workplace at productive levels after a painful loss and will need the supervisor's understanding.

Review the Four Tasks of Mourning to determine how you or someone else can facilitate addressing the appropriate tasks. Employees who remain in denial for an extremely long period (who never really address Task 1) will need special help. One employee refused to report to her new supervisor and remained attached to her former boss. In time, she agreed to employee assistance counseling and eventually reported to the new supervisor.

10. **Create a ritual celebration for welcoming new members of a group, unit, or department. A ceremony as part of a lunch meeting will symbolize the new identity of the group and its members.**

Problem: When the organization fails to note the passing of an era—an ending—it becomes more difficult for affected employees to let go.

Comment: One manager described employees who were so resistant to letting go of the old group, name, and location that they bluntly refused to leave their old offices—even though the new offices were in elegant new buildings. In another company, people physically held on to their desks when the relocation coordinator walked through the door. An organization-wide ritual to "pass the mantle" to the newly formed group would have helped these employees face the future. For example, employees can create a new logo or emblem that includes aspects of the old symbols.

Encourage employees of the new work group to take on the challenges of change. Assist this by establishing "buddy" or mentor relationships for a 30- to 60-day period. Provide opportunities for the new group to share the meanings of the changes to them.

Rituals to help new employees establish their new identity can be both formal and informal. The goal is to enable employees to withdraw their attachment to the old and reinvest it in the new work environment. As this happens, healing takes place.

Grief Support During Organizational Transition

Organizations must provide employees the following elements for adequate grief support:

> ➤ Frequent, accurate information

> ➤ Time to grieve

> ➤ Support services, including rituals, support groups, and counseling

> ➤ Training in new work skills and grief support skills

To help employees understand what to expect from the grief reaction to change in the workplace, consider holding a four-hour transition grief support workshop, led by a qualified in-house staff person or by an outside consultant. It is important that the workshop leader use the helpful listening skills presented earlier in part.

Half-Day Employee Transition Grief Support Workshop

This workshop should be in a quiet, undisturbed space. Be sure to provide time for participants to express their feelings. This is an opportunity for employees to learn about workplace grief and what to expect in their own grief process. Here is a proposed agenda using the exercises in this book:

1/2 hour	Introduction to change-loss grief Leader presents, using the material from the part titled "The Complexities of Grief"
1 hour	Individuals complete exercises: "The Many Faces of Loss" and "Your Change-Loss History"
1/2 hour	Discussion of individual responses to "Your Change-Loss History" exercise
3/4 hour	Group exercise: "Workplace Change Stories" and "Sharing the Meanings of the Change" After an introduction by the leader, participants relate their workplace change-loss experiences. The leader facilitates a discussion of feelings generated by the changes and follows up by explaining what types of support people need for their feelings.
1/2 hour	Application to workplace, and homework: Create a good-bye ritual or other "letting go" activity and have a group discussion of what support is available to employees.

A Final Statement

Everyone grieves differently, and the timetable for mourning varies from person to person. Grief is not right or wrong—it is just a normal human reaction to loss. The loss can be a death, serious illness, or physical impairment, or another traumatic change in a person's life circumstances. Managers, human resources staff, co-workers, and others can help this process along by attending to the human needs for letting go and facilitating new beginnings.

We typically resist change. Familiar routines, procedures, organizational relationships, and workplace culture are hard to let go of. Yet given the right individual and group support, loss can bring positive outcomes. When handled in the best way, workplace change-loss can create a gift of new possibilities for both the employee and the organization.

The organization or "family" can create new traditions for a new culture.

Someday people will look back at the times of workplace upheaval and sincerely acknowledge the difficulty of the changes. They will also give thanks for the courage of people who had no choice but to make changes in their work, in their lives, and in themselves.

A P P E N D I X

Appendix to Part 2

Comments & Suggested Responses

Test Your Recall on the Nature of Grief

1. survival

2. self-image, dreams, health

3. a. loss

   b. threat of loss

   c. something we never had or never will have

Appendix to Part 4

Comments & Suggested Responses

Helpful Listening

Although there is no single perfect way to respond to a grieving person, the following are some suggested helpful listening responses to the matching numbers above:

1. *"It really gets you angry to be kept in the dark."*

   "You really get mad when you don't know what's happening."

   "It's upsetting not to know."

2. *"You really seem sad about the people who are gone."*

   "This place really depresses you now."

3. *"Sounds like you're scared about your future."*

   "That's a big worry for you, isn't it?"

4. *"You're scared something else might happen."*

Additional Reading

Autry, James A. *Love and Profit: The Art Of Caring Leadership*. NY: Perennial Currents, 1992.

Bonet, Diana. *The Business of Listening*. Boston, MA: Thomson Learning/Course Technology, 2001.

Bowlby, John. *Loss: Sadness and Depression*. NY: Basic Books, 1982.

Bridges, William. *Transitions: Making Sense of Life's Changes*. NY: Perscus Books Group, 1980.

Bridges, William. *Managing Transitions: Making the Most of Change*. NY: Perseus Books Group, 2003.

Buono, Anthony F. and James L. Bowditch. *The Human Side of Mergers and Acquisitions*: *Managing Collisions Between People, Cultures, and Organizations*. Frederick, MD: Beard Books, 2003.

Covey, Stephen R. *The 7 Habits of Highly Effective People: Powerful Lessons in Personal Change*. NY: Free Press, 2004.

Everly, George S. and Jeffrey M. Lating. *A Clinical Guide To the Treatment of the Human Stress Response*. NY: Plenum Publishing, 2002.

Gowing, Marilyn K., et al. *The New Organizational Reality: Downsizing, Restructuring, and Revitalization*. Washington, D.C.: APA Books, 1998.

Jeffreys, J. Shep. *Helping Grieving People—When Tears Are Not Enough: A Handbook for Care Providers*. NY, London: Brunner-Routledge, 2005.

Kübler-Ross, Elisabeth. *On Death and Dying*. NY: Scribner, 1997.

Lord, Janice Harris. *No Time For Goodbyes: Coping with Sorrow, Anger, and Injustice After a Tragic Death*. Oxnard, CA: Pathfinder Publishing, 2000.

Mills, D. Quinn. *Rebirth of the Corporation*. NY: John Wiley & Sons, Inc., 1991.

Nadeau, Janice Winchester. *Families Making Sense of Death*. Thousand Oaks, CA: Sage Publications, 1997.

Neimeyer, R. "The Language of Loss: Grief Therapy as a Process of Meaning Reconstruction." *Meaning Reconstruction and the Experience of Loss*. Washington, D.C.: American Psychological Association, 2001.

Noer, David M. *Healing the Wounds: Overcoming the Trauma of Layoffs and Revitalizing Downsized Organizations*. San Francisco: Jossey-Bass, 1995.

Pritchett, Price. *After The Merger: The Authoritative Guide for Integration Success*. NY: McGraw-Hill, 1997.

Quick, James Campbell, et al. *Preventive Stress Management in Organizations*. Washington, D.C.: APA Books, 1997.

Scott, Cynthia D. and Dennis T. Jaffe. *Managing Change at Work.* Boston, MA: Thomson Learning/Course Technology, 2004.

Scott, Cynthia D. and Dennis T. Jaffe. *Managing Personal Change.* Boston, MA: Thomson Learning/Course Technology, 2004.

Woodward, Harry and Steve Buchholz. *Aftershock: Helping People Through Corporate Change.* NY: John Wiley & Sons, Inc., 1987.

Worden, J. William. *Grief Counseling and Grief Therapy: A Handbook for the Mental Health Professional.* Springer, NY: Springer Publishing Company, 2001.

NOTES

Now Available From

THOMSON
™
COURSE TECHNOLOGY

Books • Videos • CD-ROMs • Computer-Based Training Products

If you enjoyed this book, we have great news for you. There are more than 200 books available in the *Crisp Fifty-Minute™ Series*. For more information contact

Course Technology
25 Thomson Place
Boston, MA 02210
1-800-442-7477
www.courseilt.com

Subject Areas Include:

Management
Human Resources
Communication Skills
Personal Development
Sales/Marketing
Finance
Coaching and Mentoring
Customer Service/Quality
Small Business and Entrepreneurship
Training
Life Planning
Writing